SPIRITUAL CROSS TRAINING

13-Week Bible Study

The Book of
JAMES

Terrence Chandler-Harrison

Townsend Press

You were the first person to refer to me as "scholar" and you always set

excellence as the standard for all my pursuits. You cultivated my passion for

education and inspired me to become an educator.

Thank you, Magister Bertram E. Cox.

And to the wisest man I know—my Papa John.

For years, you have instilled in me the importance of making disciples of Jesus.

That steadfast charge greatly inspired this work. Thank you, PJ.

CONTENTS

Series Overview

Cross training is an intense fitness regime that uses rigorous activities to sculpt and strengthen the bodies of individuals. Cross-training sessions combine unique exercises that train various parts of the body, which reduce injury and fatigue. Essentially, the goal of cross training is to improve the overall performance of individuals. Similarly, the goal of Christian discipleship is to improve the overall quality of believers. Indeed, every follower of Jesus is expected to remain spiritually fit—this is only accomplished when believers consistently commit themselves to cross training.

James addressed the book of James to the twelve tribes of Israel who were scattered across Gentile nations among Gentile people. James penned his letter to encourage the newly converted disciples to maintain their spiritual fitness even as they were scattered among those who appeared to be spiritually unfit. James ardently admonished the believers not to allow their circumstances to cause them to forsake their Christian teachings.

Through his letter, James reminded the twelve tribes about several vital Christian virtues that every believer must practice in order to maintain true spiritual fitness. Hence, the book of James serves as a cross-training manual for all believers. Similarly, this thirteen-week series on the book of James will serve as cross training and will help strengthen Christian virtues in all believers.

How to Use This Study

This Bible study provides a creative guide for churches and small groups to explore what it means to practice and maintain Christian virtues in an increasingly un-Christian culture. This series is structured so that it can be used in a variety of different settings; however, this series is intended to help develop Christian disciples through Christian virtues. Therefore, we have written this series with the underlying assumption that it is being shared with a group of Christians or those who are interested in Christian discipleship. Through thirteen sessions of study, you and your group will participate in cross training. You will walk through the book of James and examine thirteen lessons that will introduce thirteen virtues that every Christian must practice in order to maintain spiritual fitness. The thirteen virtues include

    11/30 1. **Joy** (James 1:2-4)

    2. **Wisdom** (James 1:5-8)

    3. **Maturity** (James 1:9-11)

    4. **Discipline** (James 1:13-15)

    11/30 5. **Gratefulness** (James 1:16-18)

    6. **Self-control** (James 1:19-21)

    7. **Obedience** (James 1:22-25)

    8. **Equality** (James 2:1-13)

    12/1 9. **Compassion** (James 2:14-20, 26)

    10. **Gentleness** (James 3:1-12)

    12/1 11. **Prioritization** (James 5:1-6)

    12. **Patience** (James 5:7-12)

    13. **Prayer** (James 5:13-20)

Each lesson is equipped with a student outline, which includes a lesson guide, word study, discussion questions, a memory verse, and review questions. We have also included lesson guides for teachers/facilitators at the end of the book. We pray that all of you are transformed as you walk through this series.

Now, let's start cross training!

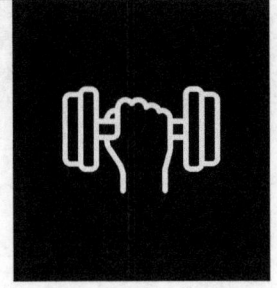

Introduction

Paul reminds us that our bodies are temples of the Holy Spirit. Therefore, we are to manage and maintain our bodies as dwelling places of God.

I have a confession: I have not always managed my body as a dwelling place of God. As a teenager, I struggled with major weight problems. I was not just chubby—I was slowly destroying my temple. I remember having breathing issues, sleeping issues, and self-esteem issues. After several years of poor health decisions, I made a life change by taking control of my health, changing my diet, and committing myself to fitness. Now, I look better, I feel better, and I *am* better.

More than our physical fitness, it is important for believers to maintain spiritual fitness. If we honestly examine our lives, I'm sure we would all agree that there are areas in our lives where we are spiritually unfit.

Fortunately, I believe that in the same way that people successfully follow key health principles to improve physical fitness, disciples can implement key heavenly principles to improve overall spiritual fitness.

As you study this series, embrace the challenge of applying God's heavenly principles as you undergo cross training. Second, commit yourself to perpetually implementing those principles in your life each and every day. Lastly, celebrate your spiritual growth and share these principles with all you encounter.

May this series richly bless all of you!

SESSION 1

I Have Joy

Lesson Focus Verses: *James 1:2-4*
Memory Verse: *Nehemiah 8:10*
Christian Virtue: *Joy*

My brothers and sisters, whenever you face trials of any kind, consider it nothing but joy, because you know that the testing of your faith produces endurance; and let endurance have its full effect, so that you may be mature and complete, lacking in nothing. **(James 1:2-4)**

Lesson Question

How can I obtain complete joy?

Lesson Objective

To understand that joy is a gift that God gives to believers that allows them to remain positive and poised while enduring trials and testing.

Warm Up!

Merriam-Webster defines the word *happiness* as "obsolete, good fortune and prosperity. A state of well-being and contentment. A pleasurable or satisfying experience."

Discussion Question
What makes you happy?

 *We seek happiness*

Stretch It!

James addressed this book to the twelve tribes of the Diaspora—the dispersion. These were twelve tribes of Israel, who were scattered across Gentile nations among Gentile people. James wrote this letter to the early Jewish Christians residing in Gentile communities outside of Palestine. The intention of this book is to speak to people who are in the world but who should never be of the world. James begins by analyzing and addressing the attitudes, attributes, and actions of the believers.

James opened this portion of the letter with a command: *count it all joy.* James commands believers to have the right attitudes.

James 1:2—count it all joy . . . .

We not only need the right _____; we also need the right _____.

Word Study

Complete *(holoklēros)*: complete in all respects; faultless—free from sin; completely whole.

Endurance *(hypomonē)*: steadfastness; constancy; patience; perseverance.

Joy *(chara)*: extreme and overwhelming gladness; uncontrollable cheerfulness; calm delight.

Perfect *(teleios)*: finished; a fully grown adult; complete in all areas of life.

Our attitudes affect our . . .

(1) _____

(2) _____

Discussion Question

What does it take for believers to have right attitudes?

In order for us to acquire complete joy, we must ask ourselves, "Where is our attention?"

Our attention affects our attitudes, and our attitudes affect our actions and attributes.

James said, "Count it all joy whenever you face trials of any kind" (see James 1:2).

Here, *trials* can mean both "tests" and "temptations."

God _____, and Satan (the Enemy) _____.

Exercise It!

Set 1: Do Not Let Problems Stop You

"My brothers and sisters, whenever you face trials of any kind, consider it nothing but joy." (James 1:2)

. . . WHEN you face trials of any kind.

Here, James warned believers about the inevitability of problems. Yes, we all will face problems—it is a part of life. No one should ever believe that they are exempt from trials and tribulations. Furthermore, no one should ever believe that "righteous living" would free them from experiencing the ills of the world.

Remember the words of our Lord Jesus: "For [God] makes his sun rise on the evil and on the good, and sends rain on the righteous and on the unrighteous" (Matthew 5:45).

Discussion Question
How do you handle and respond to problems?

James used a fascinating phrase to illustrate the severity of the problems that we might face. James wrote, *"when you face trials of any kind,"* or as the KJV puts it, *"when you fall into divers temptations."* This phrase is the same phrase used in Luke 10:30 describing the tragedy that happened to the man in the parable of the Good Samaritan. Here, the depiction is of a person who fell among thieves—surrounded by thieves who wished to rob that person, strip that person, beat that person, and kill that person.

Essentially, James encourages believers to find joy even when they are surrounded by people who wish to rob them, strip them, beat them, and kill them. In fact, James encourages believers to *count it all joy*—pure joy—complete, intense, unalloyed joy, when they are surrounded by near-death experiences.

Discussion Question
How would you have handled being in a situation like the beaten man's in the parable of the Good Samaritan?

 **Cool Down**

How has life caused you to deactivate the joy of the Lord in your life? This week, identify those areas and ask God to restore your joy so that you might triumph past those tribulations.

So, why should we count it all joy when we face trials of any kind?

Set 2: Let God Produce Perseverance
James offers a reason for the authorization of our problems. In verse 3, James says we "count it all joy" (KJV) because we know the *testing of your faith produces endurance.*

• **Testing** *(dokimion)*:

Here, James used the word *testing*. *Testing* has an OT nuance where it refers to the refining of silver and gold—to make genuine/pure. The word *testing* is the word *dokimion*. William Barclay argues that this word was "used for sterling coinage for money, which is genuine and unalloyed." Hence, "the aim of testing is to purge us of all of our impurities."

• **Endurance** *(Hupomone):*

Moreover, according to James, the testing produces *endurance.* The word *endurance* implies *unwavering patience and perseverance.* The Greek word is *Hupomone,* which depicts one who is able to relentlessly persevere during suffering and even victoriously vanquish all suffering. The etymology of this Greek word means "remaining under." It paints the picture of a person successfully carrying a heavy load for a long time. It's not simply the ability to bear things during testing; it's the ability to turn the testing into greatness and glory.

Therefore, for James, our testing is meant to refine our faith and to produce perseverance in us.

Only those who have experienced the joy of the Lord can remain positive and poised—even in the face of persecution, while God produces perseverance.

Discussion Question

How has God used testing and tribulation to refine your faith and to produce perseverance in you?

It is true that God uses our adversity to develop us; luckily, our adversity won't last always.

"In this you rejoice, even if now for a little while you have had to suffer various trials, so that the genuineness of your faith—being more precious than gold that, though perishable, is tested by fire—may be found to result in praise and glory and honor when Jesus Christ is revealed" (1 Peter 1:6-7).

Our persecution is _____, but our joy is _____.

 **Cool Down**

What have you learned during your moments of testing? How have you grown as a result of your testing? This week, take time to celebrate and to thank God for the spiritual growth that you have experienced.

So, what reward does a believer receive for persevering during persecution?

Set 3: God Prospers after God Produces

James concludes this pericope by encouraging his audience about how God not only uses our trials to produce perseverance, but God also uses our trials to prosper us.

Discussion Question

How do you think God should prosper those who count it all joy whenever they face trials of any kind?

James writes, "Let endurance have its full effect, so that you may be mature and complete, lacking in nothing" (James 1:4).

According to James, God prospers believers by making them ...

(1) _____

(2) _____

(3) _____

Therefore, we find joy in knowing that God will perfect us, complete us, and equip us through our trials.

• **Perfect** *(teleios):*

God prospers us by making us perfect. This Greek word for "perfect" is *teleios*, which means "perfection towards a given end." This word can also mean "perfect," "fit," "mature," or "fully grown."

John Paul Heil analyzed this word and explains that the word *perfect* "carries a connation not only of maturity through growth but of completeness or wholeness within a context of moral and ethical worship acceptable to God. In the biblical tradition, a sacrifice to be worthily used in worship had to be perfect in the sense of being whole and integral, without any defects."

• **Complete** *(Holokleros):*

God also prospers us by making us complete. The Greek word for "complete" is *holokleros*, which means *"entirely perfect in every way."* This word was usually used to describe the fitness of priests and sacrificial animals in the presence of God. Here, neither priest nor sacrifice is disfigured or covered with disqualifying blemishes.

• **Sufficient** *(Leipesthai):*

Lastly, God prospers us by making us *sufficient.* The Greek word is *leipesthai*—derived from the root *leipō*, which means *to be destitute, to lack, to be wanting, and to fail.* This word is usually used to describe a soldier and/or army that has been defeated, has surrendered, or has conceded due to the failure to reach the established standard. Here, this word implies that God—through our testing—will ensure that we are never people that experience defeat due to failure to adhere to the established standard.

 **Cool Down**

In what areas would you like God to make you perfect, complete, and sufficient? Have you made yourself available for God to prosper you in these areas? This week, specifically ask God to make you perfect, complete, and sufficient in those areas and commit yourself to finding joy during the process.

Final Stretch

1. Have you fully embraced the joy of the Lord?

_____

_____

_____

_____

2. What changes will you make to ensure that you always operate with the joy of the Lord?

_____

_____

_____

_____

3. How do you feel knowing that God always produces perseverance during your persecution?

_____

_____

_____

_____

SESSION 2

Wisdom:
The Missing Ingredient

Lesson Focus Verses: *James 1:5-8*
Memory Verse: *Psalm 11:10*
Christian Virtue: *Wisdom*

If any of you is lacking in wisdom, ask God, who gives to all generously and ungrudgingly, and it will be given you. But ask in faith, never doubting, for the one who doubts is like a wave of the sea, driven and tossed by the wind; for the doubter, being double-minded and unstable in every way, must not expect to receive anything from the Lord. **(James 1:5-8)**

Lesson Question

Why should everyone possess wisdom?

Lesson Objective

To understand that wisdom is a gift that God generously gives to those who seek it. We must learn how to passionately and purposefully seek after wisdom from God in faith—without doubt.

 **Warm Up!**

Discussion Question

What ingredients does it take to make a great cake?

 **Stretch It!**

In the opening of this letter, James offered a command to the believers scattered across Asia Minor. James wrote, *count it all joy whenever you face trials of any kind*, because testing of your faith produces endurance, because you know that the testing of your faith produces endurance; and let endurance have its full effect, so that you may be perfect and complete, lacking in nothing (see James 1:2-4).

However, in our text today—even after stating that with joy, we will be made *perfect, lacking nothing*—James seems to imply that there might still be something missing in us. James wrote, "If any of you is lacking in wisdom . . . ."

Word Study

Doubting *(diakrinō)*: to withdraw, to desert, or to hesitate; to separate one's self in a hostile spirit; to oppose; strive with dispute; contend; to be at variance with one's self.

Generously *(haplōs)*: simply; openly; frankly; bountifully; sincerely.

Ungrudgingly *(oneidizō)*: without defame; taunt; reproach; revile; or suffering.

Wisdom *(sophia)*: broad and full of supreme intelligence; human and divine knowledge acquired by acuteness and experience.

The missing ingredient is _____.

So, what's the secret to finding joy in the midst of the trials? What's the secret to counting it all joy when you find yourselves in divers temptations—surrounded by thieves, robbers, and murderers who wish to kill you, strip you, rob you, beat you, and leave you to die? What's the secret to rejoicing when God allows you to go through the fire? It's when one has the wisdom to recognize who is always in complete control.

The ingredient that every believer must possess is _____!

Exercise It!

Set 1: Seek Wisdom

Again, James writes, "If any of you is lacking in wisdom, ask God" (James 1:5). Here, James is clear that believers must seek wisdom in their lives.

Discussion Question

How would you define wisdom?

Wisdom is _____

_____

Now, there is a difference between *knowledge* and *wisdom*.

Knowledge versus Wisdom

Knowledge: exposure (What I've learned by what I have heard or seen)

Wisdom: experience (What I've learned by what I have lived)

You see, wisdom has little to do with education, wit, rational intelligence, or smarts. Wisdom is a skill that is developed through experience that helps an individual make the best rational decision in the midst of irrationality and irrational people.

Discussion Questions

Who is the wisest person you know? Why?

2 CHRONICLES 1:7-12; I KINGS 3:5-15

May we all look to the life of Solomon as a model of wisdom seeking. Second Chronicles 1:7-12 and I Kings 3:5-15 both record two occurrences where Solomon encountered God's presence. And when prompted with these words, "Ask for whatever you want me to give you," Solomon replied, "Give me wisdom, knowledge and discernment."

Discussion Question

Why would Solomon seek wisdom for his life?

The benefits of wisdom include . . .

(1) _____

(2) _____

(3) _____

Discussion Question

How have words of wisdom helped you navigate through life?

Since wisdom is an invaluable asset, we must all seek after wisdom for our lives like treasure. The Proverbs writer offered, "[make] your ear attentive to wisdom and [incline] your heart to understanding; if you indeed cry out for insight, and raise your voice for understanding; if you seek it like silver, and search for it as for hidden treasures—then you will understand the fear of the LORD and find the knowledge of God" (Proverbs 2:2-5).

Cool Down

Have you prioritized the necessity of wisdom in your life? How can you become more intentional in your pursuit of God's wisdom? Remember, without wisdom, it becomes very difficult to garner the discipline needed in order to manage all that we obtain. This week, center yourself in devotion in prayer and assess the areas where you need God to give you wisdom.

Set 2: Ask for Wisdom

James not only advised his audience about the importance of wisdom, but he also reminded believers that God is the source of all wisdom. James writes, "If any of you is lacking in wisdom, ask God."

Discussion Question

Why should we ask God for wisdom?

The Proverbs writer reminded us, "For the LORD gives wisdom; from his mouth come knowledge and understanding; he stores up sound wisdom for the upright" (Proverbs 2:6-7a).

Psalm 111:10 informs us, "The fear of the LORD is the beginning of wisdom." Here, this "fear" is not operated by the tyrannical hand of God that seeks to push, punish, and bring pain; it's a fear that causes one to be fully dependent on God at all times. You see, this wisdom—this fear—is one that causes a person to only make decisions after first consulting God.

Unfortunately, some people fear that God ignores them and that God will not grant them wisdom. Hence, many people fail to ask God for wisdom or to consult God for direction in their lives.

Discussion Question

When have you been afraid to ask God for something? What do you believe is/was the source behind your hesitation/apprehension?

James debunks this notion by reminding his audience that God not only gives wisdom but God also graciously gives wisdom to those who seek it.

James writes, *if any of you is lacking in wisdom, ask God,* who gives to all generously and ungrudgingly, and it will be given you.

James is clear—God gives . . .

(1) _____

(2) _____

According to James, God first gives generously. The word used here for "generously" is *haplōs*, which means *simply, openly, frankly, bountifully, sincerely*. We can boldly seek wisdom from a God who simply, openly, frankly, bountifully, and sincerely desires to give to those who ask for wisdom.

• **Generously** *(haplōs)*:

Second, James contends that God gives ungrudgingly. The word used here for "ungrudgingly" is *oneidizō*, which means *without defamation, taunting, reproach, revile, or suffering.* Therefore, we confidently approach a God who will never defame, taunt, reproach, revile, or add suffering to anyone who seeks wisdom.

• **Ungrudgingly** *(oneidizō)*:

Discussion Questions

How do you feel knowing that God desperately desires to give wisdom to you? How empowered are you now to approach God's throne boldly and confidently?

 **Cool Down**

How much do you trust God to direct your life? Are you fully dependent on God? This week, trust God's direction and ask God for wisdom to follow those directions.

Set 3: God Gives Wisdom

Discussion Question

How do you think God should prosper those who count it all joy whenever they face trials of any kind?

With this new confidence, James invites his audience to boldly ask God for wisdom. However, James cautions us to ask for wisdom correctly—with the right spirit.

James warns in verses 6-8, "But ask in faith, never doubting, for the one who doubts is like a wave of the sea, driven and tossed by the wind; for the doubter, being double-minded and unstable in every way, must not expect to receive anything from the Lord."

James commands his audience to ask, but to ask in faith. James is clear: since we know that God does not give grudgingly, but God gives generously, then we should all approach and make our appeals to God in faith. Essentially, James is charging believers to bring faith to our faithful God— the one who always works on our behalf.

James continues by admonishing his audience to rid themselves of doubt. James pens in verse 6, "But ask in faith, never doubting."

Discussion Question

How have you allowed doubt to overwhelm you?

For James, doubters are double-minded and unstable in every way, and are those who must never expect to receive anything from the Lord.

James continues by warning us that the one who doubts is like a wave of the sea, driven and tossed by the wind. This depiction illustrates a person who is as choppy as waves on a tempestuous sea. These faithless doubters are easily moved by present problems and predicaments. These faithless doubters are controlled by circumstances. These faithless doubters lack stability and security—they move wherever the winds of life take them.

James conversely urges believers to activate their faith during prayer. Our faith activates all the promises that are found in the Word of God. Moreover, when we pray for wisdom—by faith, then God grants our request.

 **Cool Down**

Has doubt postponed progress in your life? This week, commit yourself to removing all doubt and ask God for the wisdom to pray by faith and to walk by faith.

Set 4: Apply Wisdom

After we have asked for wisdom, we must be willing to apply the wisdom that God gives. Below are four essentials that will help guide to the application of God's wisdom.

(1) _____ (Psalm 1:1-3)

(2) _____ (Proverbs 6:6)

(3) _____ (Proverbs 13:20)

(4) _____ (Proverbs 12:15)

Final Stretch

1. How often do you routinely and carelessly maneuver through life without consulting God?

_____

_____

_____

_____

2. How can you become more intentional about seeking God's wisdom in your life?

_____

_____

_____

_____

3. What adjustments do you need to make to remove all doubt from your life?

_____

_____

_____

_____

SESSION 3

Overcoming Shallowness

Lesson Focus Verses: *James 1:9-11*
Memory Verse: *Proverbs 11:4*
Christian Virtue: *Maturity*

Let the believer who is lowly boast in being raised up, and the rich in being brought low, because the rich will disappear like a flower in the field. For the sun rises with its scorching heat and withers the field; its flower falls, and its beauty perishes. It is the same way with the rich; in the midst of a busy life, they will wither away. (James 1:9-11)

Lesson Question

Why shouldn't we spend our lives desperately pursuing possessions on Earth?

Lesson Objective

To understand that all earthly possessions are temporary—they all will fade away. However, if we pursue God, we will receive the permanent riches of God's glory, which are found in heaven.

 **Warm Up!**

Discussion Question

What would you buy if you won the lottery, a jackpot, or a game show prize?

 **Stretch It!**

In this portion of James's letter to the twelve tribes of the Diaspora—the dispersion—James offers a warning about the obsession with materialism. James knew the difficulty of maintaining true spirituality while living in a superficial, materialistic world. In fact, if we are honest, we all can admit that not much has changed since the days of James—our author. Many churchgoers are mesmerized by the messages of music, media, and ministries that perpetuate the myth: the more one possesses, the more one is valued.

Word Study

Boast *(kauchaomai)*: rejoice; glory; vaunt.

Lowly *(tapeinōsis)*: lowness; low estate; spiritual abasement; humiliation.

Raised up *(hypsos)*: on high; high station; high rank; elevation; immense dignity.

Rich *(plousios)*: wealthy; abounding in material resources.

Consequently, most people find value in what they possess. Therefore, the more they possess, the more they feel valued and supposedly the higher their self-worth. However, in the words of Jesus, "one's life does not consist in the abundance of possessions" (Luke 12:15).

Discussion Question

Where/in what do you find value?

Many people seek _____ _____ of God, not _____ _____ of God.

We forget that the greatest blessing—our most valuable gift—is salvation. Certainly, we are rich because we have access to life everlasting with the Everlasting One.

Exercise It!

Set 1: Boast about Godly Riches

James began this portion of his letter by addressing a specific people. In verse 9, James pronounces, "Let the believer who is lowly. . . ." James refers to his audience as "lowly," which depicts lowness, low estate, and humiliation. This audience is believed to be Messianic Jews who were subject to discrimination and marginalization due to their beliefs and practices while subsequently dealing with hardship, bigotry, and economic disparities due to injustices. James Martin contends that these people were poor or lowly because of their religious choice to follow Christ. Douglass Moo claims that this "poor or lowly" phrase *depicts a people who are of little significance in the world's evaluation—people who are oppressed by the world.*

Hence, in this text, James seeks to usurp the superficial standards of the world by shifting the focus of the followers of Christ. Here, James desires to develop the maturity (wisdom) of his audience by teaching them to never be consumed with the present—temporal—materialistic pursuits; but they are to always walk confidently in the hope and assurance of the future.

Discussion Question

How difficult is it to remain positive and faithful to God when you experience the "lows" of life?

If we are honest today, we would all agree that it is difficult to accept "lowly" living when Scripture is saturated with so many financial promises. Some include

• The wealth of the wicked is laid up for the righteous (see Proverbs 13:22).

• The blessings of the Lord maketh you rich and adds no sorrow (see Proverbs 10:22).

• God will supply all our needs according to God's riches in glory (see Philippians 4:19).

Dan McCartney argues that although James's trajectory rails on the deceitful practices of the wealthy, the main problem here is not wealth per se, but certain attitudes toward wealth, both on the part of the wealthy themselves and on the part of those who pander to them.

James invites the believer who is lowly to boast. Here, the word *boast* means "to rejoice, glory, and vaunt." This is a call to proudly and joyfully celebrate. Boasting is only negative when it is self-centered. However, James invites believers to boast about the glory of God.

Never boast about _____. We only boast about _____.

Discussion Question
James, why should the lowly boast?

According to James, the believer who is lowly boasts in being raised up. For James, the believer who is lowly will eventually be raised up. Here, *raised up* means "to be elevated on high, to be elevated on a high station, to be elevated to a high rank, with immense dignity." You see, believers do not boast about earthly riches; believers boast about godly riches.

Do not boast about _____ riches; believers boast about _____ riches.

Believers know that Earth is not their final destination and that God has promised them riches that extend beyond cars, clothes, cash, cards, and homes.

Therefore, James encouraged believers who feel low to boast—to rejoice, glory, and vaunt—because they know that God will raise them to high stations and high ranks with immense dignity.

 **Cool Down**

How do you imagine that God will reward you for faithfully serving God while on Earth? This week, every time you start to feel bad about your circumstances, boast in the fact that you are loaded with the riches of God's glory.

Set 2: Never Trust the Temporal
James continues with a very striking warning in verse 10: "And the rich in being brought low, because the rich will disappear like a flower in the field."

Here, James reminded his audience that all of our lives are impermanent, and nothing that we possess on Earth will remain forever. In a real sense, James declares that no one can take earthly riches with them when they die. Ergo, our trust should never be put in temporal things like money and personal assets.

Discussion Question

What earthly possession do you find yourself cherishing the most?

In order to punctuate the severity of trusting temporal things, James offers these word: the rich will be brought low and the rich will disappear like a flower in the field (see verse 10). Now, the language that James uses is what makes this claim ironically fascinating. James cautions that the rich will be brought low. Here, James used the same word "low" to describe the plight of the rich, which he used to illustrate the status of the believers in verse 9.

This is ironically fascinating because James seems to imply that the temporary predicament of believers on Earth as "low" would shift eschatologically, and the temporary status of the believers would become the permanent status of the rich who put their trust in temporal things.

In lieu of James's notion, Friedrich Nietzsche posits that the gospel reverses values and undermines the true order of society. On Earth, the rich appear to be blessed; however, after death, those who have been redeemed will be overflowing with the riches of God's glory. Even Jesus concurred with these sentiments when He warned, "The last will be first, and the first will be last" (Matthew 20:16).

Thus, since temporal—earthly—possessions are fleeting objects, we all must put our trust in the God who promises to shower us with the permanent riches of God's glory.

 **Cool Down**

Be honest: how would you feel and react if you lost all your earthy possessions today? This week, ask God for the discipline and maturity to assist you in gaining freedom from any obsession of temporal things. And ask God to help you value and pursue the riches of God's glory.

Set 3: Invest in Eternity

In order to convince and compel his audience to invest in eternity, James wrote in verse 11, "For the sun rises with its scorching heat and withers the field; its flower falls, and its beauty perishes. It is the same way with the rich; in the midst of a busy life, they will wither away."

In these two verses, James makes two things very clear:

(1) _____

(2) _____

Discussion Question

How do you feel knowing that you will die one day and that you will not be able to take your earthly possessions with you?

You see, it is true that we will all die and we will all face judgment from God in heaven. James knew that the accumulation and acquisition of earthly wealth would never help us during Judgment Day. The author of Proverbs warned us about this difficult reality as well with these words: *wealth is not profitable on a day of wrath, but righteousness rescues from death* (see Proverbs 11:4).

This is why James was pleading with his audience to rid themselves of the shallowness of superficialities. James's plea is simple: invest in eternity before it is too late.

Beloved, our only true _____ is found in our _____.

We are given an eternal investment plan for believers in 1 Timothy 6:17-19.

According to I Timothy 6:17-18, we invest in eternity . . .

• _____

• _____

• _____

• _____

• _____

I TIMOTHY 6:19

 **Cool Down**

How well have you made investments for your eternal stay? This week, make a decision to intentionally invest in your eternal portfolio.

Final Stretch

1. Have you been valuing earthly possessions over the riches of God's glory?

   _____

   _____

   _____

   _____

2. Should you scale back on how much money you spend on physical possessions?

   _____

   _____

   _____

   _____

3. Have you ensured that you will spend eternity with God in heaven once you die?

   _____

   _____

   _____

   _____

SESSION 4

Fighting Temptations

Lesson Focus Verses: *James 1:13-15*
Memory Verse: *1 Corinthians 10:13*
Christian Virtue: *Discipline*

No one, when tempted, should say, "I am being tempted by God"; for God cannot be tempted by evil and he himself tempts no one. But one is tempted by one's own desire, being lured and enticed by it; then, when that desire has conceived, it gives birth to sin, and that sin, when it is fully-grown, gives birth to death. **(James 1:13-15)**

Lesson Question

How do I overcome temptation?

Lesson Objective

To understand that believers must fight to control their desires in order to conquer temptation.

 **Warm Up!**

The word *temptation (peirasmos)* means "enticement or to put to the test." It is the state of being where one is attracted to say, do, or feel what is wrong.

Discussion Question

What are your temptations/guilty pleasures?

 **Stretch It!**

In our text today, James addressed a community of Messianic Jewish believers who were subject to the times of that day. They loved Jesus but were very susceptible to the ills of the world. The same is true presently—believers love God but fight against the two greatest threats to our spiritual vitality: *self* and *Satan*.

Our two greatest threats:

(1) _____

(2) _____

This is why Jesus told us to pray in Matthew 6:13 (KJV): "and lead us not into temptation, but deliver us from evil." Here, we are taught to pray and ask God to remove us from the evil of Satan and the influences of evil within ourselves. Every day, we all should ask God for the power to resist our temptations and to remove ourselves from the areas of our temptations.

Word Study

Desire *(epithymia)*: a lust, craving, or longing for what is forbidden.

Enticed *(deleazo)*: to bait; catch by bait; to allure or deceive.

Temptation *(peirasmos)*: an experiment, attempt, or trial.

Tempted *(peirazo)*: to try whether a thing can be done; to attempt an endeavor; to test or make trial.

James wrote to the believers—the twelve tribes of the Diaspora—in order to warn some and remind others about the dangerous, adverse effects that come upon believers that are overtaken by temptations. James explicitly exposed the root cause and driving force of temptation: sin.

Sin means _____ .

Two types of sin:

(1) _____

(2) _____

The first are sins of commission. Sins of commission are ACTIONS that we willfully, voluntarily, and intentionally COMMIT that disregard and disobey the Word of God and the walk of God—demonstrated by Jesus Christ.

The second are sins of omission. Sins of omission are ACTIONS that we willfully, voluntarily, and intentionally OMIT that disregard and disobey the Word of God and the walk of God—demonstrated by Jesus Christ.

Two questions we must ask are these:

(1) What are we doing that God's Word clearly states we should not be doing? (COMMISSION)

(2) What should we be doing that God's Word clearly states we should be doing? (OMISSION)

Exercise It!

Set 1: Do Not Make Excuses

Discussion Question

Who/what do you blame when you make mistakes?

One of the biggest problems with overcoming temptation is the "blame game." Instead of accepting responsibility for our weaknesses and mistakes, we prefer to blame others.

We blame God, others, the media, biology, the devil, and the list goes on…

Discussion Question

When was the last time you tried shifting the blame for a mistake you made? Why did you choose to blame someone else? Why is it so hard to accept responsibility for sin?

In a rebuttal to these excuses, James offered, "no one, when tempted, should say, 'I am being tempted by God'; for God cannot be tempted by evil and he himself tempts no one" (James 1:13).

God _____ and Satan _____.

However, notice that James does not place responsibility on God nor does James blame Satan; James doesn't even acknowledge Adam as the source of sin. It is true that we are subject to the fall of Adam, wherein we have sinful natures; however, that does not necessarily mean we have to act on our impulses or natures.

James puts the onus of responsibility on each individual. James made it very clear: we play a role in our own mistakes.

Discussion Question

Why shouldn't people place blame on God and Satan?

We fail because we spend more time pointing blame instead of owning up to our mistakes. Moreover, Christian maturity is about recognizing flaws, owning up to and learning from mistakes, and making the necessary changes for improvement.

 **Cool Down**

In what areas of your life have you made excuses for your actions? This week, commit yourself to take full responsibility for your mistakes and choose to make the necessary changes to improve your life as a disciple of Jesus.

Set 2: Do Not Be Moved by What Excites You

So, if we are to take responsibility for our sins, then we must recognize the source of our sin.

Discussion Question

What do you believe is the source of your sin? How have you seen this manifest in your life?

"But one is tempted by one's own desire, being lured and enticed by it; then, when that desire has conceived, it gives birth to sin, and that sin, when it is fully grown, gives birth to death." (James 1:14-15)

Contrary to popular belief, sin does not just fall out of the air. Sin is processed through phases. Let us now analyze the different phases/stages of sin.

Phases/Stages of Sin:

(1) Desire

(2) Deception

(3) Disobedience

(4) Death

Desire

> "One is tempted by one's own desire." (James 1:14)

We all have many legitimate desires: affirmation, attention, affection, approval, acceptance, and appreciation. Tony Evans argues that these desires become a problem when Satan tempts us to meet a legitimate desire in an illegitimate way. Our normal God-given desires become carnal and corrupt when we contaminate them by seeking to fulfill them in worldly and not "wordly" ways.

Satan knows all humans struggle with controlling desires because desires are God-given. Therefore, our adversary seeks to manipulate how we satisfy our desires. You see, Satan wants your desires to dominate you; however, God's Holy Spirit empowers you to master your desires. The first step and most important key to mastering your desires is transparency/honesty. All believers must transparently evaluate their lives and must be honest about their weaknesses. Only when believers are honest about their weaknesses are they able to begin the steps to conquering their temptations.

Discussion Questions

Take a moment and be honest: What are your desires? What are your weaknesses? How often do you give in to them?

Deception

"Being lured and enticed by it." (James 1:14)

Notice James's wording. James claims that believers are lured and enticed by our desires. The word *lured* has a root that means "bait." The word *lure* depicts a fish that is lured to bait and then caught by a hook. The word *enticed* means "trapped" and depicts a bear that is enticed by food in a trap.

This text reminds us that uncontrolled desires lure and entice people into deception. The goal of Satan's deception is to offer believers temporary desirables that carry permanent consequences.

Discussion Question
How have you been deceived by your desires?

Disobedience

"then, when that desire has conceived, it gives birth to sin." (James 1:15)

Disobedience is inevitable when believers are overtaken by the deception of their desires. It is here where believers make mistakes and some even justify their actions with excuses. Before long, believers who engage in disobedient acts become comfortable with living outside of the will of God. Remember: one small mistake always leads to another. Therefore, it is important to consistently resist temptation no matter how trivial and harmless the opportunity may seem.

Discussion Question
What are some consequences you have faced as a result of your disobedience?

Death

"And that sin, when it is fully grown, gives birth to death." (James 1:15)

James warned that the sin of disobedience brings death. Paul reminds us that the price for sin is always death (see Romans 6:23). This *death* is not limited to physical death; sometimes, believers can experience mental, financial, spiritual, and relational deaths.

Discussion Question

What things have died in your life as a result of disobedience?

 **Cool Down**

In what areas of your life have you consistently fallen victim to temptations? Have you spent time evaluating the root of the problem? This week, identify the things that excite you and draw you into temptation. Lastly, ask God for the discipline to remove yourself from the areas of your weakness.

Set 3: Do Not Miss the Exit

Death can stand as a consequence for disobedience, but there is a way to overcome temptation.

Discussion Question

How can we avoid being overcome by temptation?

1 CORINTHIANS 10:13

We must never forget that God always makes a way of escape. The problem is that we see the exit sign and we avoid it or even ignore it.

Remember: the exit of deliverance always comes through the Word of God.

We must . . .

(1) _____ the Word.

(2) _____ the Word.

(3) _____ the Word.

 **Cool Down**

How many times have you ignored the stop signs and flashing red lights from God? This week, reflect on the warnings that have been revealed to you through the Word of God. Additionally, commit yourself to fully seeking and obeying God's instructions.

Final Stretch

1. What temptation(s) give(s) you the most trouble?

_____

_____

_____

2. Are there any temptations that you have ignored?

_____

_____

_____

3. How do you feel knowing that God works with you and warns you before you fall?

_____

_____

_____

4. How will you respond to God's ways of escape?

_____

_____

_____

5. How would you advise a person who wishes to overcome temptation?

_____

_____

_____

SESSION 5

Be Grateful

Lesson Focus Verses: *James 1:16-18*
Memory Verse: *James 1:17*
Christian Virtue: *Gratefulness*

Do not be deceived, my beloved. Every generous act of giving, with every perfect gift, is from above, coming down from the Father of lights, with whom there is no variation or shadow due to change. In fulfillment of his own purpose he gave us birth by the word of truth, so that we would become a kind of first fruits of his creatures. **(James 1:16-18)**

SESSION

5

Small-group Bible Study

Lesson Question

Why should I live my life full of gratitude?

Lesson Objective

To understand that we should be grateful that we share intimacy with a loving God who freely supplies all our needs.

 **Warm Up!**

Discussion Question

For what are you most grateful?

 **Stretch It!**

James's letter was intended to combat the carnal influences that impacted the believers scattered across the Diaspora.

One of the major influences of that day—as it is today—was an overwhelming sense of self-glory, fueled by the toxins of humanism. People wholeheartedly believed that they were the reason for all their success and sustainability.

Discussion Question

Whom do you credit for your success?

Word Study

Deceived *(planaō)*: to wander, go astray, be led in error, stray from truth.

From above *(anōthen)*: the very first or the beginning; from the higher place.

Generous *(dosis)*: a benefit; that which is good, or of good constitution or nature; that which is useful, excellent, distinguished, upright, and admired.

Gift *(epithymia)*: a bounty; benefaction; or bestowment.

In order to debunk the flawed notions of ultrahumanism, James offered a warning in James 1:16: "Do not be deceived, my beloved." Here, the word *deceive* means "to wander, go astray, be led in error, stray from truth." James offered this warning to prevent his audience from sinking deep into the abyss of humanism. Moreover, James wanted his audience to never forget that there was a greater force at work with them and within them—a force that drives and guarantees their success.

Exercise It!

Set 1: Be Grateful that God Is Your Source

In this section, James was very clear: we all possess gifts. James used the word *gift*, which indicated a bounty, benefaction, or bestowment. James emphasized gifts that were given graciously. Beloved, cars, clothes, homes, degrees, certifications, jobs, businesses, spouses, and children are all gifts that we did not earn nor do we deserve.

Discussion Questions

- *What gifts do you possess, and which gifts do you value the most?*
- *Where did/do these gifts come from?*

Society teaches that hard work always pays off. We live by the belief that those who work hard are those who enjoy the nice things.

We typically accredit our success to . . .

(1) _____

(2) _____

(3) _____

Discussion Question

Have you ever experienced burnout because you felt like you were working alone?

In order to dispel these myths, James confirms that it (our gifts) comes from above. The phrase "from above" connotes the very first or the beginning and from the higher place. James wanted his audience to know that God is the very first—the beginning—and heaven, the higher place, is where God resides. Therefore, our gifts come from God. Undeniably, God is the source of our supply. Indeed, everything that we have, everything that we are, and everything that we will ever become will come from the hands of God.

Now, James is not attempting to fully discredit the hard work and sacrifices made by individuals in their pursuits of success; however, James wants his audience to recognize the one who equips and empowers individuals to achieve success and to experience the blessings of life.

Indeed, God is both _____ and _____.

Discussion Question
How does God give?

James 1:17—"Every generous act of giving, with every perfect gift, is from above."

Here, James informs his audience that God gives . . .

(1) _____

(2) _____

To James, we ought to be grateful that God—who is our source—gives generously and perfectly.

 **Cool Down**

How often do you attempt to take credit for your own success and for the blessings in your life? How do you feel knowing that God is the source of all your supply and that God works with you to ensure that you experience the many blessings of life? This week, take time to acknowledge God's presence and ask God for the discipline to step back as God works on your behalf.

Set 2: Be Grateful that God Is Sovereign

Discussion Questions

How do you know that God is the source? How can we trust that God gives generously and perfectly?

James explained why God has been and why God will always be the source of our success and supply in verse 17; he writes, "Every generous act of giving, with every perfect gift, is from above, coming down from the Father of lights, with whom there is no variation or shadow due to change."

Here, James enlightened his audience concerning the *distribution headquarters* and the *distributor of our gifts*. James made it very clear that all our gifts, both generous and perfect, come from above—which come down from the Father of Lights.

First, James made his audience aware of the distributor of our gifts—the Father of Lights. This phrase "Father of Lights" that James used was intended to validate the sovereignty of God. Here, James reminded his audience that God is the sovereign one who separated dusk from light and day from night in the book of Genesis. James wanted his listeners to know that God is not just light; more importantly, God is the Father of Lights. By doing this, James sought to prove the sovereignty of God. For James, the same way that God was the source of light in Genesis is the same way that God is the source of life for all of us today.

James rallies all of us to express our gratitude for a God who is and will always be the sovereign one who supplies all our _____.

Discussion Question

How do you feel knowing that God is the Father of Lights?

To further punctuate this claim, James used the phrase "coming down" as a means to highlight the distribution center of our blessings. James is unwavering in the fact that all our gifts come down from heaven. In short, heaven is the distribution center for all our blessings. This is why David passionately penned the words, "I lift up my eyes to the hills—from where will my help come? My help comes from the LORD, who made heaven and earth" (Psalm 121:1-2). What a joy and privilege it is for us to have the unrestricted right to pray to God—the Father of Lights—in heaven, the distribution headquarters for all our gifts.

Now, what's fascinating about James's usage of the phrase "coming down" is the verb tense in which he speaks. The phrase "coming down" is used in the present participle tense, which implies continuous or repeated action. Therefore, according to James, God continuously and repeatedly showers us with gifts from above. In fact, Malachi testifies to this truth in that God promises to open the windows of heaven for us and to pour down an overflowing blessing that we will not even have room enough to receive (see Malachi 3:10). Thus, we are to be grateful that we know and serve a God—the Father of Lights—who continuously and repeatedly opens up windows of heaven and pours down overflowing blessings into our lives.

Discussion Question

Have you ever had someone to make a promise to you and then change his or her mind? How did that make you feel?

I believe it is safe to assume that we all have been there before—we all have had people to offer us broken promises. In response to these unfortunate circumstances, James connects some assurance to God's promise for the believer. James pens that God—the Father of Lights—has no variation or shadow due to change. James wanted his audience to know that God does not operate like humans. God will not make a promise to sovereignly supply all our needs, only to renege.

Never forget: what God _____, God _____.

Therefore, we are to be grateful that not only does God shower us continuously and repeatedly, but also God never changes.

 **Cool Down**

When was the last time you paused to recognize the sovereign, supplying hand of God in your life? Now that you know that God is the Father of Lights—the one who sends down gifts from above—what expressions of gratitude do you owe God? This week, rejoice that you share intimacy with the Sovereign Supplier. Also, make a commitment to intentionally direct your prayers toward heaven—the distribution headquarters of your blessings.

Set 3: Be Grateful that God Sent the Son

James concluded this portion of Scripture by reminding his audience of the most important gift that God has ever given the world. James writes in verse 18, "In fulfillment of his own purpose he gave us birth by the word of truth." James calls this gift the "Word of Truth." John reveals the identity of the Word of Truth in John 1. John reports, "In the beginning was the Word, and the Word was with God, and the Word was God. He was in the beginning with God. . . . And the Word became flesh and lived among us, and we have seen his glory, the glory as of a father's only son, full of grace and truth" (John 1:1-2,14).

From this insight, we confirm that the Word of Truth is Jesus. Therefore, our greatest gift is Jesus—the Son of God—the Word of Truth. God loved us enough to give us His very best—His Son—so that we would become a kind of first fruits of his creatures (see verse 18). In fact, God so loved the world that he gave his only Son, so that everyone who believes in him may not perish but may have eternal life (see John 3:16).

We are grateful that

(1) God is the _____.

(2) God gives the _____ _____.

(3) God gave us the_____.

We therefore can have confidence in the fact that God will supply our needs since we know that God gave us His greatest gift—God's Son.

Cool Down

How much do you value the gift of God's Son? In what areas should your faith increase? This week, acknowledge the areas where your faith in God is weak. Commit yourself to remembering the great sacrifice of Jesus and use that as fuel to power your faith.

Final Stretch

1. Have you fully surrendered to God? What keeps you from fully trusting God as the source of your supply?

_____

_____

_____

_____

2. What prevents you from trusting the sovereignty of God?

_____

_____

_____

_____

3. How confident are you in God now that you know that God freely gave you His best gift?

_____

_____

_____

_____

SESSION 6

Pressure Points

Lesson Focus Verses: *James 1:19-21*
Memory Verse: *James 1:19*
Christian Virtue: *Self-control*

You must understand this, my beloved: let everyone be quick to listen, slow to speak, slow to anger; for your anger does not produce God's righteousness. Therefore rid yourselves of all sordidness and rank growth of wickedness, and welcome with meekness the implanted word that has the power to save your souls. **(James 1:19-21)**

Lesson Question

Why must we be careful with our words?

Lesson Objective

To understand that the mastery of self-control in speech is an essential virtue for Christian discipleship.

 **Warm Up!**

Discussion Questions

Have you ever spoken too soon? Have you ever said something in the moment that you really did not mean? Have you ever said something you wish you could take back?

 **Stretch It!**

The necessity and mandate for self-control in speech runs throughout our entire Bible. This topic is addressed well more than 130 times in the Bible. In fact, self-control in speech was one of the strengths of Jesus. Jesus did not say what was on His mind at all times; Jesus practiced self-control in speech. Isaiah tells us that even while Jesus endured the Cross, He never said a mumbling word. Surely, if Jesus—God in the flesh—could practice self-control in speech while in pain, we should as well.

In the book of James, the writer is relentless in the quest to build up mature disciples of Jesus Christ. James is clear: mature disciples of Jesus Christ are those who practice self-control in speech.

Discussion Question

Why is self-control in speech so important for believers?

Word Study

Anger *(orgē)*: temper; wrath; indignation; vengeance; violent passion; movement or agitation of the soul; impulse; desire; any violent emotion.

Listen *(akouō)*: to attend to, consider what has been said; to understand; to comprehend.

Rid Yourself *(apotithēmi)*: put off; lay aside; lay down; cast off; lay apart.

Welcome *(dechomai)*: to receive favorably or to grant access to a visitor with hospitality; take up, take hold, and take with hand; to accept; to approve; to give ear, embrace, and bear.

Wickedness *(kakia)*: malice; ill will; desire to injure; evil; trouble.

There is a strong correlation between ...

(1) _____

(2) _____

(3) _____

You see, our words can either _____ or _____.

Exercise It!

Set 1: Practice Self-control

Discussion Question

What is your first reaction when someone says something that triggers one of your pressure points?

James summoned his audience with an alternative to poor reactions as a result of aggravated pressure points. James writes in verse 19, "You must understand this, my beloved: let everyone be quick to listen, slow to speak, slow to anger."

Here, James introduced a three-step self-control formula:

(1) _____

(2) _____

(3) _____

In our pursuit of mastering self-control, James first encourages believers to be quick to listen. Here, the word *listen* means "to attend to, or consider what has been said." It means "to comprehend and to understand." James not only encouraged believers to be listeners but also commands believers to be rapid listeners—those who swiftly run to listen. James encouraged believers to be great communicators—those who listen attentively.

James urged believers not only to be listeners but also to be learners. James writes, "Let everyone be quick to listen, slow to speak." By listening and refraining from immediately speaking, one is able to listen and learn from the individual that is talking. Here, the believer seeks to understand someone before he or she seeks to be understood. This quality allows the believer to be guided by a golden principle: process before proclamation—or, as most of us learned, *think before you speak.*

Discussion Questions

• *How difficult is it for you to listen before you speak?*
• *Why is it important to process before you speak?*

James cautions that those who immediately speak in the moment without rumination are usually the ones who allow their agitated pressure points to produce anger within. Thus, James instructs us to "be quick to listen, slow to speak, slow to anger." Here, the word *anger* implies *wrath, indignation, vengeance, violent passion, any violent emotion, and the movement or agitation of the soul, impulse, and desire.* Thus, we are always overtaken with anger when our pressure points are agitated.

 **Cool Down**

In what areas do you need to practice more self-control? Have you discovered your triggers? How has your lack of self-control caused you to lose control of your anger? This week, identify our pressure points and practice processing before proclaiming.

Set 2: Produce God's Righteousness

Discussion Question

Why must we control our anger?

First, we look foolish when we "fire off" on people. A person who fails to restrain himself or herself during a heated encounter best displays "firing off."

It is a fool who cannot control anger; the wise person restrains it (see Proverbs 29:11).

Discussion Question

Have you ever scorned or laughed at a person who was uncontrollably angry? What made them look so foolish? Have you ever acted that foolishly?

James 1:20—"For your anger does not produce God's righteousness."

Again, this "anger" is more than crossed arms and deep exhaling. This "anger" is wrath, indignation, vengeance, violent passion, any violent emotion, and the movement or agitation of the soul, impulse, and desire. And, for James, *it does not produce God's righteousness.*

You see, our _____ are never _____.

And our actions of anger never produce the righteousness of God. Moreover, our actions of anger are never given by God or guided by God. Therefore, believers must practice self-control if they wish to produce the righteousness of God.

 **Cool Down**

Consider a time when you allowed your actions to cause you to act foolishly. How unproductive were those actions? How much damage did you cause? Whom did you hurt? This week, recall those occurrences and repent to God for your allowing your actions to cause you to be counterproductive. Commit yourself to change. Ask God to guide you in your speech and in your actions so that you may produce God's righteousness.

Set 3: Part Ways with Your Past

James 1:21—"Therefore rid yourselves of all sordidness and rank growth of wickedness, and welcome with meekness the implanted word that has the power to save your souls."

We must _____ ways with our _____ ways.

James's first objective in parting ways with our past is by *ridding ourselves of all sordidness and rank growth of wickedness.* James commands believers to "rid themselves" of the past. "Rid" indicates "to put off, lay aside, lay down, cast off, and lay apart." It depicts one who has stripped oneself—literally taken off dirty clothes or shedding old skin like reptiles.

James commands believers to rid themselves of sordidness and wickedness. This term *sordidness* is a derivative of the Greek word *rhupos*. It can mean extreme filth—usually used to describe dirty, soiled garments. It can refer to extreme grime as with filthy clothes that are stained, muddy, and soiled. When this word is used in the medical sense it means excess wax in ears. Douglas Moo argues that here, James uses this word to convey *the deeper meaning of moral defilement, of spiritual stains of the soul.*

Additionally, James invited believers to rid themselves of rank growth of wickedness. Here, "wickedness" indicates *malice, ill will, evil, trouble and an immense desire to injure.* However, when James adds rank growth of wickedness it indicates something that has been sitting and staining for a long period of time. Hence, here, James commands believers to rid themselves of malice, ill will, evil, trouble, and an immense desire to injure.

Now, the most fascinating part of this charge is the verb tense that James uses. Here, the aorist temporal participle of "rid" implies that these actions have already taken place. Therefore, James is really saying, since you have already *rid yourselves of all sordidness and rank growth of wickedness,* don't put those filthy clothes—those filthy ways of living–back on.

We will always fall victim to agitation of our pressure points, so long as we continue to wear our past ways of living.

Discussion Question

What are some unproductive and ungodly ways of talking and reacting that you used to display when you were younger (in age and in spiritual maturity)?

James concludes with an alternative to wearing sordidness and rank growth of wickedness. James writes, "welcome with meekness the implanted word that has the power to save your souls" (see verse 21).

Here, *welcome* means "to receive favorably or to grant access to a visitor with hospitality." It also means "to take up, take hold, and take with the hand." Lastly, it means "to accept, to approve, to give ear, embrace, and bear."

Essentially, James instructs his audience to *welcome the Word of God* that has already been planted in our lives.

James reminds every believer that we all have been given assistance in our pursuit of maintaining self-control in speech. Our aid is found in the Word of God. Therefore, when we rid ourselves of our past ways and welcome the Word that has been planted in us, then we will always be successful in maintaining self-control in speech.

 **Cool Down**

How often do you consult the Word of God when a pressure point is triggered? How often do you ignore the Word of God when a pressure point is triggered? This week, devote yourself to searching for Scripture that speaks about self-control and commit yourself to memorizing and applying those Scriptures in your life.

Final Stretch

1. How much do you value the Word of God as the guide in your life?

    _____

    _____

    _____

    _____

2. How committed are you to mastering self-control in speech?

    _____

    _____

    _____

    _____

3. What changes do you need to make to ensure that you react less during your moments of anger?

    _____

    _____

    _____

    _____

Practice What You Preach

Lesson Focus Verses: *James 1:22-25*
Memory Verse: *John 15:7*
Christian Virtue: *Obedience*

But be doers of the word, and not merely hearers who deceive themselves. For if any are hearers of the word and not doers, they are like those who look at themselves in a mirror; for they look at themselves and, on going away, immediately forget what they were like. But those who look into the perfect law, the law of liberty, and persevere, being not hearers who forget but doers who act—they will be blessed in their doing. **(James 1:22-25)**

Lesson Question

Why should believers practice the Word of God?

Lesson Objective

To understand that God equipped us with the Word of God so that we might receive the Word, reflect on the Word, and replicate the Word. God promises to bless all who not only hear the Word but also who practice the Word.

 **Warm Up!**

Discussion Questions

- *What physical qualities do you most like about yourself?*
- *What physical qualities do you wish you could alter about yourself?*

 **Stretch It!**

The book of James is addressed to a community of newly converted Messianic Jews who were scattered across Gentile nations among Gentile people. James wrote to this community to assist them in maintaining their faith by strengthening the core essentials of discipleship.

In our text today, James immediately prompts this community of believers about the importance and necessity of the Word of God. James is clear: the Word of God is mandatory for Christian development and maturity. Moreover, all believers must value the Word of God. Truly, the Word of God is the foundation of our faith. And the Word of God must be central in the lives of all believers.

Word Study

Doers *(poiētēs)*: a maker, producer, performer, or author; one who replicates.

Look *(katanoeō)*: consider; behold; perceive; discover; perceive; remark; to observe fully; to consider attentively; to fix one's eyes or mind upon something/someone.

Look *(parakyptō)*: to stoop down with head bowed forward and body bent to inspect something carefully; to inspect something long enough to become acquainted with it.

Persevere *(paramenō)*: to continue; to abide; to remain beside—always near; to survive and to remain alive.

Discussion Question

Why should people value the Word of God?

Jesus reminds us that man (woman) must not live on bread alone but on every word that comes from the mouth of God (see Matthew 4:4). Indeed, all believers should live by every word that comes from God.

James wanted his audience to know emphatically that it is impossible to live a rich and productive life without a serious appreciation for the Word of God.

In our text today, James offered three mandates for believers:

(1) We must _____ the Word of God.

(2) We must _____ the Word of God.

(3) We must _____ the Word of God.

Exercise It!

Set 1: Receive the Word

James makes a very intriguing postulation in verse 22. James commands, "Be doers of the word, and not merely hearers." Here, James's implied assumption is that his audience is comprised of "hearers" of God's Word. James made this assumption because hearing the Word of God is a standard for discipleship. Paul reminds us that faith comes by hearing, and hearing by the Word of God (see Romans 10:17). Truly, we *fortify our faith* through the Word of God. David endorses this theory with his declaration: the Word of God is the lamp unto our feet and light unto our paths (see Psalm 119:105). Indeed, all believers are expected to be hearers of God's Word.

We receive the Word through . . .

(1) _____

(2) _____

Discussion Question

How have you been impacted as a result of hearing God's Word?

James's audience was a community of Jewish Christians. They believed and accepted Jesus as the true Messiah, but still were very much indoctrinated with Jewish custom and ritual. Hearing Scripture—mainly the Torah and Pentateuch—the Word of God, read formerly out loud was an essential element of religious ritual. Indeed, the reading of the Torah was sacred. In fact, many young Jewish boys still read and recite the Torah during bar mitzvahs as public displays of transition in worship. Therefore, James's audience was not only familiar with the Word of God but also could recite the Word of God.

James did not discourage the reception and recitation of God's Word. Conversely, James elevated the expectation for his audience. James commanded believers in verse 22, "But be doers of the word, and not merely hearers who deceive themselves." Here, the word *doers* implies a *maker, producer, performer, or replicator.* James ordered believers to become makers, producers, performers, and replicators of God's Word. This charge is given in the present imperative tense which denotes a continuous, habitual command. Therefore, this charge was a call for a lifelong commitment. Believers must commit themselves to "doing the Word." You see, it was not enough for believers to receive God's Word; believers must respond to God's Word. Indeed, our attentiveness to God's Word should always influence action on our part. Jesus warned that those who hear His words and do not act on them build their houses on sand (see Matthew 7:26).

Cool Down

How consistent are you in positioning yourself to hear the Word of God? How much stronger and more stable would your life be if you spent more time receiving and responding to the Word of God? This week, commit yourself to strategically positioning yourself to hear the Word of God.

Set 2: Reflect on the Word

James used a unique mirror metaphor to expose the nature of individuals who refuse to respond to God's Word. James contends that if anyone is a hearer of the Word and not a doer, he is like a man looking at his own face in a mirror (see verse 23).

The Word of God is the _____ into our lives.

The Word of God—just like mirrors—should force believers to look at their reflections in order to measure and monitor the spiritual status of their lives.

Craig Blomberg posits, "Mirrors in the ancient world were very different from our modern crystalline inventions. Mirrors weren't as available nor were they used as frequently as they are today. Generally made of polished bronze or copper, mirrors produced dim and warped reflections." The mirrors rested horizontally on tables so that people who wished to see their reflections had to bend and look down. This metaphor reminds all believers that the Word of God is a mirror into our lives and we must therefore intensely examine our lives every time we encounter the Word of God. Essentially, God desires for all believers to reflect on the Word of God after they receive the Word of God.

Discussion Questions

Why is it important to reflect on the Word of God? What have you learned about yourself as you have reflected on God's Word?

Sadly, our society is filled with far too many "selfies" and very little self-reflection. With this in mind, James detailed the actions of ignorers of God's Word. According to James, there are individuals "who look at themselves in a mirror; for they look at themselves and, on going away, immediately forget what they were like" (verses 23-24). Here, the word *look* indicates one that "considers, beholds, perceives, and remarks. It is one who observes fully, and considers attentively. It is one who fixes his/her eyes or mind upon something/someone." Thus, those who are hearers only—those who are ignorers of God's Word—are those who fully and attentively behold themselves through the mirror of Scripture and then immediately walk away forgetting what the Word of God revealed to them.

Here, James exposed the negligence of those who ignore God's Word. You see, the "forgetfulness" that James referenced in this text was not actually *ignorance*; it was blatant *insubordination*. To look into the mirror of God's Word and immediately walk away is ludicrous. These actions are akin to people who: wake up in the morning, see sleep crust in their eyes, dried saliva on their faces, and their hair in an undesirable tornado tumbleweed fashion, and walk away without grooming themselves. These individuals have become comfortable and complacent with flagrant flaws.

"Forgetfulness" is not _____; it is blatant _____.

The Hebrew writer forewarned us, "Indeed, the word of God is living and active, sharper than any two-edged sword, piercing until it divides soul from spirit, joints from marrow" (Hebrews 4:12).

The Word does not _____ ; the Word is designed to _____.

Cool Down

Indeed, God's Word exposes our flaws and empowers us to make necessary changes in our lives. What flaws has God revealed to you during your reflection time? Are there areas that you are neglecting? This week, study God's Word and ask God to explicitly reveal the flaws in your life. Afterward, ask God for the desire and discipline to be obedient to God's Word.

Set 3: Replicate the Word

James concluded this pericope by presenting his audience with the proper response to God's Word. James suggests this in verse 25: "But those who look into the perfect law, the law of liberty, and persevere, being not hearers who forget but doers who act—they will be blessed in their doing."

Here, James is clear that doers of God's Word are those who act after encountering God's Word. Notice the precise actions of the doers of God's Word. these individuals look into the perfect law, the law of liberty, and persevere.

Now, the interesting thing about this portion of the text is James's word usage. Earlier, James spoke about the hearers who look at themselves through the mirror of Scripture and walk away. Yet, when James speaks about doers who look into the perfect law—the law of liberty, the Word "look' is slightly different in the Greek. Here, doers not only *stoop down with bowed heads and bent bodies to inspect the Word of God carefully*, but also inspect the Word of God long enough in order to become acquainted with it. Also, doers "persevere," which implies one who *continues, abides, and remains closely beside the Word of God.* Therefore, believers are doers of the Word that are called to inspect the Word of God long enough in order to

become acquainted with it. Additionally, believers are doers of the Word that are expected to remain close beside the Word of God.

According to James, believers who look into the perfect law, the law of liberty, and persevere act on the Word of God. Beloved, God desires for all people to act on God's Word.

We must therefore . . .

(1) _____ God's Word.

(2) _____ God's Word.

(3) _____ God's Word.

God's primary desire is for all people to replicate God's Word. In fact, God promises to bless those who replicate the Word of God. James encourages us with these words: *the doers who act will be blessed in their doing*. In short, God rewards those who replicate the Word of God. Jesus confirms His promise: "If you abide in me, and my words abide in you, ask for whatever you wish, and it will be done for you" (John 15:7).

 **Cool Down**

How motivated are you to replicate God's Word now that you know God's promises? This week, commit yourself to replicating God's Word in three ways. Remember: as you replicate, God will reward.

Final Stretch

1. How important is God's Word in your life? Are there any adjustments that you need to make to express your appreciation for God's Word?

_____

_____

_____

_____

2. What keeps you from making the necessary changes in your life after you hear the Word of God? How do you think God views your disobedience?

_____

_____

_____

_____

3. What areas of your life would be enhanced if you dedicated yourself to replicating the Word of God?

_____

_____

_____

_____

SESSION 8

Be Fair

Lesson Focus Verses: *James 2:1-13*
Memory Verse: *James 2:13*
Christian Virtue: *Equality*

My brothers and sisters, do you with your acts of favoritism really believe in our glorious Lord Jesus Christ? For if a person with gold rings and in fine clothes comes into your assembly, and if a poor person in dirty clothes also comes in, and if you take notice of the one wearing the fine clothes and say, "Have a seat here, please," while to the one who is poor you say, "Stand there," or, "Sit at my feet," have you not made distinctions among yourselves, and become judges with evil thoughts? Listen, my beloved brothers and sisters. Has not God chosen the poor in the world to be rich in faith and to be heirs of the kingdom that he has promised to those who love him? But you have dishonored the poor. Is it not the rich who oppress you? Is it not they who drag you into court? Is it not they who blaspheme the excellent name that was invoked over you? You do well if you really fulfill the royal law according to the scripture, "You shall love your neighbor as yourself." But if you show partiality, you commit sin and are convicted by the law as transgressors. For whoever keeps the whole law but fails in one point has become accountable for all of it. For the one who said, "You shall not commit adultery," also said, "You shall not murder." Now if you do not commit adultery but if you murder, you have become a transgressor of the law. So speak and so act as those who are to be judged by the law of liberty. For judgment will be without mercy to anyone who has shown no mercy; mercy triumphs over judgment. (James 2:1-13)

Lesson Question

Why is it important to practice fairness toward all people? What are the dangers of playing favoritism in the faith community?

Lesson Objective

To understand that we should always treat everyone equally. We should never alienate anyone; to do so is to contradict the law of God given to us through Jesus: love your neighbor as yourself.

 ### Warm Up!

Discussion Question

Have you ever been treated unfairly because you weren't someone's "favorite"?

 ### Stretch It!

Homer Kent asserts that "discrimination is one of the great social tensions that is present and plagues our times." All sorts of people band together to exclude others from enjoying their special privileges. Discrimination can manifest in several areas, including ethnicity, sex, class, age, and religion, to name a few. The truth is that pernicious people in power put policies in place in an attempt to restrict and remove certain "unwanted" individuals. Even casual conversations masked in personal opinion can birth and incubate seeds of hate. Such unkind conduct may not be too surprising in a world where selfishness and the protection of one's own interests are the guiding principles. However, a higher standard is expected from those who profess the Christian faith.

In our text today, James was relentless in dismantling the disease of discrimination among the believers scattered across the Diaspora. James immediately jumps in by posing a poignant question in verse 1: "My brothers and sisters, do you with your acts of favoritism really believe in our glorious Lord Jesus Christ?"

Word Study

Dishonored (*atimazō*): entreat shamefully; suffer shame; despise; to render infamous; to insult; to treat with contempt in word, deed, or thought.

Distinctions (*diakrinō*): pass judgment; to separate; to discriminate; to have a preference; to withdraw or desert one; to oppose, contend, or strive with dispute against one.

Favoritism (*prosōpolēmpsia*): partiality; respect of people; one who makes judgments by analyzing the outward circumstances of people instead of intrinsic merits; to receive someone according to their face.

Judges (*kritēs*): one who passes or arrogates to himself; an arbiter; one who administers justice; a person whose conduct is made the standard for judging another and convicting them of wrong; one who passes judgment on the character and deeds of humans and rewards accordingly, like God.

Here, James's rhetorical question is intended to penetrate the entire community and permeate the minds of the entire community. James wanted this community of believers to evaluate the ways in which they handled people.

Discussion Question

How do you handle people?

James posed this question, because the way in which we treat people reveals the way in which we represent God. Moreover, James wanted this community to know that discrimination among believers should not be present, because it does not reveal the character of God.

Exercise It!

Set 1: Discrimination Denies Godly Living

JAMES 2:1

We must take notice to how James phrased this portion of the letter. James deliberately addressed the community—the church as a whole. We must remember that all our actions represent God and God's church.

Before we continue we must recognize that we are the church.

• *Ecclesia/ekklesia:*

The church is no building; it's me, it's you, it's us—we are the church.

Tell yourself this: I am _____.

Therefore, when we look at the community in the text we cannot think of a mere institution; we must see *individuals*—ourselves.

Discussion Question

How should the church treat people?

With this perspective, let us reexamine James's words in verse 1: "My brothers and sisters, do you with your acts of favoritism really believe in our glorious Lord Jesus Christ?"

Here, James charged this church—this community of believers—with showing favoritism.

The word *favoritism* that James used carries a stronger connation than mere preference. Here, *favoritism* means "practicing partiality, having respect of people." It paints the picture of one who makes judgments by analyzing the outward circumstances of people instead of intrinsic merits. In fact, one translation reads, "one who receives another according to their face."

Here, James not only charged the believers with practicing discrimination but also rebuked the believers for these repugnant actions. In the first place, James notified the believers that discrimination denies godly living.

James asks, "Do you with your acts of favoritism really believe in our glorious Lord Jesus Christ?" (verse 1). With this question, we are reminded that discriminatory actions are not aligned with actions of true discipleship. James essentially says, "Hey, you are not acting like you believe in Jesus Christ." Indeed, those who have encountered the love of Jesus are those who should never discriminate against anyone.

 Cool Down

Remember, every action we display represents the kingdom of God. How well do you represent the kingdom of God? This week, make sure that your actions positively mirror godly living.

Set 2: Discrimination Dishonors God's People

In this move, James explicitly exposed the dangers of discrimination among the believers by displaying a clear example of blatant discrimination among believers.

James pens in verse 2, "For if a person with gold rings and in fine clothes comes into your assembly, and if a poor person in dirty clothes also comes in . . . ."

James used a scenario to convey this truth: two people come into your assembly (church). Through this scenario, James reminds all of us that church should welcome all people. The church is both haven and hospital, where all people come for hope, help, and healing. In fact, the church should strive for diversity—mirroring heaven—hence, becoming the true kingdom of God.

Here, James identified two different people: a person with gold rings and in fine clothes, and a poor person in dirty clothes.

These two people represent _____ and _____.

The first type of person is described as a person with gold rings and in fine clothes; this person represents those who are privileged. This person represents status, wealth, affluence, rank, and power. In fact, the description "with gold rings" is translated literally as "with gold fingers." This person is adorned with so much gold that his fingers appear to be gold. The indication of his gold-ring fingers indicates a royal ring, possibly with an emblem of the upper-level Roman equestrian class. This would have been a ring similar to the one that was put on the son upon his arrival in the parable of the Prodigal Son.

The second type of person that James introduced is described as a poor person in dirty clothes. The emphasis on "poor" emphasizes, *one who has been reduced to beggary or asking for alms.* This person is destitute of wealth, influence, position, power, and honor. This is a person who lives in the most severe situation of poverty and has virtually no resources.

James details a disturbing course of events in verse 3. Here, James states that although these two people enter into the same church, they are treated differently. According to this text, the assembly (church) took notice of the one wearing the fine clothes and said, "Have a seat here, please," while to the one who is poor (the church) said, "Stand there," or, "Sit at my feet." The audience learns that the assembly (church) blatantly discriminated against one person solely based on how that person looked.

Discussion Question
How would you feel if you arrived at a church that operated this way?

As a response to this travesty, James asks in verse 4, "Have you not made distinctions among yourselves, and become judges with evil thoughts?"

First, James informs us that discrimination begins with evil thoughts that cause us to make ungodly distinctions among ourselves.

Discrimination begins with _____.

Here, James used the word *distinctions*, which indicates one who passes judgment, separates, and discriminates. It is one who allows a preference to cause him/her to withdraw or desert one. It indicates one who allows a bias to oppose, contend, strive, or dispute against another.

James continues by essentially asking this community, "Do you think you are judges? Do you think you are God?" Indeed, we insult God when we attempt to play God by practicing discrimination.

It is true, as C. Freeman Sleeper posits, that the assemblies were not just places of worship and teaching; the assemblies also performed judicial and business functions. The church has always been the place that has the power to free or to enslave.

However, James condemned these acts as ungodly. Additionally, James exposed this flawed system. James explains in verse 5, "Listen, my beloved brothers and sisters. Has not God chosen the poor in the world to be rich in faith and to be heirs of the kingdom that he has promised to those who love him?"

Here, James explained that we shouldn't discriminate because we see things totally different from the way that God views them. Indeed, the Lord does not see as humans see; they look on the outward appearance, but the Lord looks on the heart (see I Samuel 16:7).

Lastly, James states in verse 6 that we dishonor the poor when we discriminate. The word *dishonor* denotes shameful treatment. It implies one who despises and insults. It paints a picture of one who renders another infamous and therefore treats one with contempt in word, deed, or thought.

Yes, discrimination dishonors God's people.

To _____ is to _____.

Jesus warned us, "Truly I tell you, just as you did not do it to one of the least of these, you did not do it to me" (Matthew 25:45).

What we do toward _____ is what we do toward _____.

 **Cool Down**

Have you been guilty of willingly or subconsciously practicing discrimination? Have you been guilty of dishonoring God's people? Did you damage someone? This week, ask God to reveal these moments to you; repent and ask God for direction to seek forgiveness and to restore the person(s) that you wounded.

Set 3: Discrimination Defies God's Word

In the last verses of this pericope, James offered a recommendation in verses 8-9: "You do well if you really fulfill the royal law according to the scripture, 'You shall love your neighbor as yourself.' But if you show partiality, you commit sin and are convicted by the law as transgressors." Here, James enlightened his audience by reminding them of their responsibility to uphold the royal law—God's law—the law of liberty. Moreover, we are to speak and so act as those who are to be judged by the law of liberty (verse 12).

Discussion Question

What does it mean to uphold God's law—God's Word?

For James, those who practice partiality—those who discriminate—sin and are convicted by the law as transgressors. Therefore, discrimination defies God's Word. Conversely, according to James, to uphold the royal law—God's law—the law of liberty means to love your neighbor as yourself. Here, James quoted directly from the words of Christ, who was asked to sum up the entire law, to explain the law, and to identify the greatest commandment. Jesus responded, "Love your God with all your mind, soul, and strength, and love your neighbor as yourself. On these two commandments hang all the law and the prophets" (see Matthew 22:38-40).

Since we know the Word of God, let us therefore speak and so act as those who are to be judged by the law of liberty.

 **Cool Down**

Indeed, the obedience of God's law, God's Word, is measured in the way in which we treat people. Therefore, how obedient are you to God's Word? Do you suffer from not extending the same grace to people that you seek from God? Remember, God examines the way in which we treat God's people. This week, ask God to help you see God's people in the way that He sees them. Also, make a commitment to treat people like you wish to treat God.

Final Stretch

1. How do you feel knowing that God views all people the same? Do you have issue with this notion? If so, why does this make you feel uncomfortable?

_____

_____

_____

_____

2. What changes do you need to make to ensure that you view and value all people as children of God?

_____

_____

_____

_____

3. Is there someone in your life who is blatantly, unjustly, and unapologetically discriminatory toward certain people? Is God leading you to correct them in love?

_____

_____

_____

_____

Faith in Action: Show It!

Lesson Focus Verses: *James 2:14-20, 26*
Memory Verse: *James 2:26*
Christian Virtue: *Compassion*

What good is it, my brothers and sisters, if you say you have faith but do not have works? Can faith save you? If a brother or sister is naked and lacks daily food, and one of you says to them, "Go in peace; keep warm and eat your fill," and yet you do not supply their bodily needs, what is the good of that? So faith by itself, if it has no works, is dead. But someone will say, "You have faith and I have works." Show me your faith apart from your works, and I by my works will show you my faith. You believe that God is one; you do well. Even the demons believe—and shudder. Do you want to be shown, you senseless person, that faith apart from works is barren? . . . For just as the body without the spirit is dead, so faith without works is also dead. **(James 2:14-20, 26)**

Lesson Question

Is faith alone enough to live a purpose-fulfilled life?

Lesson Objective

To understand that it is impossible to please God without faith. However, faith does not stand alone; faith must have action in order for it to be activated.

 **Warm Up!**

Discuss the following issues:

- Poverty
- Famine
- Drought
- Homelessness
- Sickness

 **Stretch It!**

Discussion Question

What would you do/what are you doing to help impact and eliminate these issues?

Faith is the foundation of our formation and the furtherance of our statement of belief. Faith is not only what we do, but faith is also who we are:

- Without faith it is impossible to please God. (Hebrews 11:6)

- We walk by faith, not by sight. (2 Corinthians 5:7)

- The righteous/just shall live by faith. (See Galatians 3:11, Hebrews 10:38, Romans 1:17.)

Discussion Question

What is faith?

Now faith is the assurance of things hoped for, the conviction of things not seen. (Hebrews 11:1)

Word Study

Barren *(argos)*: useless; idle; slow; free from labor—at leisure; lazy; shunning the labor that one ought to perform; unprofitable.

Dead *(nekros)*: lifeless; one that has breathed its last; deceased or departed; inactive or inoperative.

Save *(sōzō)*: make whole; heal; to restore to health; to rescue from danger or destruction; to prevent someone from experiencing injury, peril, suffering, disease, or perishing.

Works *(ergon)*: labor; deed; doing; toil; business, employment enterprise that is undertaken or occupied; anything accomplished by hand, art, industry, or mind.

Although faith is a necessity, faith does not stand alone; faith must have action in order for it to be activated.

James is addressing Christian Jews who were trained to believe that acceptance of doctrine was the ultimate sign of faith. Essentially, they believed that verbal articulation offered validation. Here, James debunked this school of thought and presented a new way of thinking about faith. For James, faith is not what you say but is found in what you show. Moreover, James does not seek to remove faith; however, James seeks to contrast two types of faith:

Two types of faith:

(1) _____ faith.

(2) _____ faith.

It is important to notice what James actually says in the opening verse of this pericope. In verse 14, James does not say "if a man has faith"; James, rather, says that if a man "SAYS" he has faith . . . ." The issue in juxtaposition is the difference between the claim of possessing faith and the actual praxis of faith.

With this statement, James indirectly exposes what one might call "faith impostors." Faith impostors are people *who proclaim faith but do not practice faith.*

James asks in verse 14, "What good is it, my brothers and sisters, if you say you have faith but do not have works?" Here, James emphasizes the importance of believers' practicing works in order to authenticate their faith. The word *works* that James used suggests "some labor, deed, doing, or toil." It also implies some business, employment, or enterprise that is undertaken or occupied. It also means "anything accomplished by hand, art, industry, or mind."

James prompts his audience to put their faith to work—to put their faith in action. James's question reveals that our *actions* activated our *faith.*

Discussion Question
Why must faith be activated with action?

(1) Faith without action does not _____ .

(2) Faith without action does not _____ .

(3) Faith without action does not _____ .

Exercise It!

Set 1: Faith without Action Does Not Protect

James posed a question for this argument in verse 14: "What good is it, my brothers and sisters, if you say you have faith but do not have works? Can faith save you?"

Here, the word *save* is not a sole soteriological term; *save* deals with protection and restoration. *Save* means "to heal, to make whole, and to restore to good health." It means "to rescue from danger or destruction." It also implies one who "prevents someone from experiencing injury, peril, suffering, disease, or perishing."

This rhetorical question was used to underscore the fact that our actions have the potential to heal, to make whole, and to restore to good health. Additionally, our actions have the ability to prevent people from experiencing injury, peril, suffering, disease, or perishing.

Moreover, our faith in God should propel us to work to ensure that others are healed, whole, and restored. This objective cannot be accomplished with mere beliefs and with mere words. Our faith requires action—an action to protect those who are hurt, harmed, and in poor health; those who are in danger and/or destruction; those who are experiencing injury, peril, suffering, disease, or perishing.

Discussion Questions

Have you ever had someone protect or save you from danger or harm? How did that make you feel? How do you view that person now?

Our commitment to protecting people displays our faith in the God that protects us, but it also demonstrates our faith in the God that empowers and equips us to help protect others.

 **Cool Down**

Is there someone in your life who needs protection? How can your faith empower you to help them? This week, ask God to reveal unto you those who need protection. Ask God to empower your faith and to adequately equip you with the resources you need in order to provide protection to those individuals.

Set 2: Faith without Action Does Not Provide

James continued by posing a hypothetical question in verses 15-16: "If a brother or sister is naked and lacks daily food, and one of you says to them, 'Go in peace; keep warm and eat your fill,' and yet you do not supply their bodily needs, what is the good of that?" With this question, James reminded believers about our responsibility to respond to those in need.

In this scenario, James painted an unfortunate reality for most people in the body of Christ. In this scenario, the faithful believers offered optimistic words to people who are naked and famished, instead of supplying their bodily needs. Here, the faith believers offered *spiritual proclamations* for *secular problems*.

Discussion Questions

How would you want people to treat you and respond to you if you were in need of food, water, shelter, and clothing? Do you respond in this same manner?

Unfortunately, the church has successfully equipped people with ecclesiastical essentials while neglecting the necessities needed in order to navigate in the world. Indeed, we have mastered proclaiming blessings, but very few people practice benevolence.

We must not only _____; we must also _____.

James pens in verse 17, "So faith by itself, if it has no works, is dead." For James, faith without action is dead faith: faith that is "lifeless, without breath, deceased, departed, inactive, and inoperative."

You see, proclamations of faith without actions fail to provide the necessary aid that activated faith releases.

Beloved, sometimes, we are called to meet spiritual needs, and sometimes, we are called to meet physical, earthly needs. Indeed, our faith journey should force us to consider spiritual needs and physical needs. In fact, when churches meet physical needs, people are more prone to meet

spiritual needs. Moreover, it is much easier to fulfill ecclesiastical responsibilities when earthly obligations are being fully met.

Discussion Questions

What is the nicest thing someone has done for you? How did that make you feel?

Never forget: our actions validate our announcements. Our faith-activated actions have longer-lasting impacts on people than mere proclamations. We must show our faith, we must prove our love, and we must do it with our actions.

Indeed, it is true that we are not saved by faith alone; however, we are saved by the faith in the works of Jesus Christ. We have faith in a God who loves us and saved us. However, we do not have blind faith. Paul reminded us that God proves His love for us in that while we were yet sinners, Christ died for us (see Romans 5:8). God showed God's love—God proved His love with works, and those actions empower our faith.

Now, it is true, our works do not save us; but our works express the faith that we have in God. Moreover, works are not the *substitute for faith*, but works are the *evidence of our faith*.

 **Cool Down**

How many people have you intentionally and unintentionally ignored who were in desperate need of the bare necessities such as food, water, shelter, and clothing? How much longer do you intend to ignore them?

Set 3: Faith without Action Does Not Produce

James concludes with a striking question in verse 20: "Do you want to be shown, you senseless person, that faith apart from works is barren?"

James is clear: faith without action is barren. Here, the word *barren* refers to something or someone that is "useless, idle, and unprofitable and slow." It implies "one that is lazy and is free from labor—at leisure." It is "one that shuns the labor that one ought to perform."

In a nutshell, James argued that we are unproductive when our faith announcements are not matched with faith actions. Our words, messages, and prayers are useless and unproductive until our faith is activated by action.

Discussion Question

How can we make our faith live?

James offered in verse 18, "But someone will say, 'You have faith and I have works.' Show me your faith apart from your works, and I by my works will show you my faith."

You see, our *works of faith* help our *witness of faith.* Our "faith in action" not only confirms our faith, but it also convinces those whom we have helped to practice faith in God as well. In a real sense, people have to *SEE our faith,* so we must *SHOW our faith.*

In a real sense, we have to _____ what we _____.

Jesus warned in Matthew 7:15-20, "Beware of false prophets, who come to you in sheep's clothing but inwardly are ravenous wolves. You will know them by their fruits. Are grapes gathered from thorns, or figs from thistles? In the same way, every good tree bears good fruit, but the bad tree bears bad fruit. A good tree cannot bear bad fruit, nor can a bad tree bear good fruit. Every tree that does not bear good fruit is cut down and thrown into the fire. Thus you will know them by their fruits."

Here, Jesus reminded us that _____ validates _____.

Discussion Question

What faith fruit are we supposed to produce?

Jesus enlightens us: "By this everyone will know that you are my disciples, if you have love for one another" (John 13:35).

Therefore, the fruit of our faith is *love.*

Our faith should empower us to produce actions of love every single day. The fruit of our faith in God is revealed in our displays of love for people. And love is best seen through action. Therefore, let our love be displayed through compassion, service, empathy, sacrifice, benevolence, hospitality, mercy, and grace.

 **Cool Down**

In what areas of your life are you unproductive? How can you ensure that your faith is producing the fruit of love? This week, commit yourself to producing the fruit of faith in every area of your life.

Final Stretch

1. Has your faith been inactive lately? What contributions can you make to put your faith back in action?

_____

_____

_____

_____

2. Do you maintain good works, or are your good works occasional and weak? What changes do you need to make to ensure that your faith in God is seen in your works?

_____

_____

_____

_____

3. How has your faith increased with the knowledge that God protects, provides, and prospers you?

_____

_____

_____

_____

SESSION 10

Tame the Tongue

Lesson Focus Verses: *James 3:1-12*
Memory Verse: *Proverbs 18:21*
Christian Virtue: *Gentleness*

Not many of you should become teachers, my brothers and sisters, for you know that we who teach will be judged with greater strictness. For all of us make many mistakes. Anyone who makes no mistakes in speaking is perfect, able to keep the whole body in check with a bridle. If we put bits into the mouths of horses to make them obey us, we guide their whole bodies. Or look at ships: though they are so large that it takes strong winds to drive them, yet they are guided by a very small rudder wherever the will of the pilot directs. So also the tongue is a small member, yet it boasts of great exploits. How great a forest is set ablaze by a small fire! And the tongue is a fire. The tongue is placed among our members as a world of iniquity; it stains the whole body, sets on fire the cycle of nature, and is itself set on fire by hell. For every species of beast and bird, of reptile and sea creature, can be tamed and has been tamed by the human species, but no one can tame the tongue—a restless evil, full of deadly poison. With it we bless the Lord and Father, and with it we curse those who are made in the likeness of God. From the same mouth come blessing and cursing. My brothers and sisters, this ought not to be so. Does a spring pour forth from the same opening both fresh and brackish water? Can a fig tree, my brothers and sisters, yield olives, or a grapevine figs? No more can salt water yield fresh. **(James 3:1-12)**

Lesson Question

Why must we tame our tongues?

Lesson Objective

To understand that untamed tongues contaminate us, control us, and contradict Christian conduct.

 **Warm Up!**

Discussion Question

How have evil words negatively impacted your life?

 **Stretch It!**

James is relentless in his quest to build mature disciples of Jesus Christ. For James, mature disciples of Jesus Christ are those who know how to tame their tongues. In our text today (James 3), James seems to backtrack in order to re-iterate a former lecture on self-control as it relates to conversations and communications. In James 1, James tells us that we must be slow to speak and quick to listen in order to produce God's righteousness; now, James commands his audience to tame their tongues.

Word Study

Perfect *(teleios)*: brought to its end; finished; wanting nothing necessary for completeness; fully grown, of full age, fully mature; a fully grown adult; complete in all areas of life.

Restless *(akataschetos)*: unruly; that which cannot be restrained.

Stains *(spiloō)*: defiles, spots, soils.

Tame *(damazō)*: curb or restrain.

James wanted the believers scattered across the dispersion to recognize the importance of taming their tongues. James's command to tame our tongues indicates having strong restraint or control. Believers must learn how to control their mouths—their words. James offered this charge because he knew the power of our words.

Discussion Question

Why must we be careful with our words?

(1) Words are _____.

(2) Words cannot be _____.

(3) Words are _____.

Discussion Question

How have the misuses of words been harmful in your life?

Before explaining the potential issues with untamed tongues, James reminded his audience that they possessed infinite influence. Indeed, we must tame our tongues, because we have *infinite influence*.

James warns both leaders and laymen about their infinite influence.

First, James offered *a warning to leaders*. James warns in verse 1, "Not many of you should become teachers, my brothers and sisters." Here, James used the word *teachers*, which has several different associations. The word can mean "master," "instructor," and even "doctor." In this context, it is most likely to be associated with the Jewish rabbis. Unlike today, teachers were held in high esteem. In the ancient Mediterranean world—our setting for this Scripture today—teachers were highly revered and highly respected. Teacher was a term of respect and endearment. This is why "rabbi" or "teacher" was the title most used to address Jesus during His day.

Yet, James warns against pursuing positions of infinite influence. Some scholars hypothesize that this was a result and a response to people who possibly desired positions of power as a means of escaping social oppressions. However, James warns that having *higher status* brings *higher stipulations*. James says, for you know that we who teach will be judged with greater strictness.

The office of rabbi/teacher was one of extreme respect but one of extreme responsibility. Teachers were the religious leaders within the community. The task of the rabbi was to learn Scripture—they had to translate Scripture accurately and transmit Scripture exactly. Essentially, rabbis were called to be carriers of the Word of God. James warned that those who carefully communicate the words of God must also carefully communicate their words to the people of God.

Second, James offered *a warning to laymen*.

James suggests in verse 2, "For all of us make many mistakes. Anyone who makes no mistakes in speaking is perfect, able to keep the whole body in check with a bridle." James made it perfectly clear: we all struggle with the taxing and tiring task of taming our tongues, and all of us make many mistakes because we fail to tame our tongues. James continues, if one is able to tame his tongue then he or she is perfect. The word *perfect* means "finished and complete in all areas, full of human integrity and virtue, fully grown, mature, and of adult age."

Mature people are those who have _____.

After reminding his audience about their infinite influence, James reveals the power of our tongues. For James, the tongue is an individual instrument that has immense impact on our lives.

Discussion Questions
So then, how impactful is the tongue? What are the adverse effects of having an untamed tongue?

Exercise It!

Set 1: Untamed Tongues Contaminate
James offers an important reminder to his audience. James states in verse 5, "So also the tongue is a small member."

The tongue is _____, but the tongue is _____.

James continued with a more explicit warning. James argues in verse 6, "And the tongue is a fire. The tongue is placed among our members as a world of iniquity; it stains the whole body, sets on fire the cycle of nature, and is itself set on fire by hell."

Here, we are warned about the immense power of the tongue. James warned that untamed tongues contaminate us.

Discussion Question
How does the untamed tongue contaminate?

For James, the untamed tongue contaminates us because . . .

(1) The untamed tongue _____.
   (The tongue is placed among our members as a world of iniquity.)

(2) The untamed tongue _____.
   (It stains the whole body.)

(3) The untamed tongue _____ .

    (It sets on fire the cycle of nature.)

Discussion Question

How have you witnessed uncontrolled words contaminate communities?

Essentially, what James wants believers to know is that we may not be able to avoid the positive and negative impacts of our words. However, believers can make disciplined decisions to reduce toxics that spew from untamed tongues.

Let us remember these words from the book of Proverbs: "Death and life are in the power of the tongue, and those who love it will eat its fruits" (Proverbs 18:21).

 **Cool Down**

Have you been guilty of contaminating your family, marriage, ministry, or workplace due to toxic words? Repent to God for these actions, seek forgiveness from those individuals, and make a commitment to contribute positive, life-breathing words in your communities.

Set 2: Untamed Tongues Control

Discussion Question

How influential and impactful have words been in your life?

James submits in verses 3 and 4, "If we put bits into the mouths of horses to make them obey us, we guide their whole bodies. Or look at ships: though they are so large that it takes strong winds to drive them, yet they are guided by a very small rudder wherever the will of the pilot directs."

Here, James correlates the controlling power of an untamed tongue with a horse's bit and a ship's rudder. Horses and ships were two main forms of transportation in those days. The small individual bit in the mouth controlled strong horses and small rudders placed at the rear-controlled solid ships. James declares that just as those small bits and small rudders determine stallions' and ships' destinations, what we say can very well be the vehicles of your destination.

Our words can either direct us toward our _____ or our _____ .

We learn from James that when we fail to *control our words*, we become *controlled by our words*.

James pleaded with these believers about the necessity of practicing and maintaining self-control in communication. William Barclay warns, "Let people before they speak, remember that once words are spoken it is gone from their control." *Yes, once we speak words, they can never be erased from the corridors of people's minds—they are permanent.*

Continuing, James argues the following in verses 7-8: "For every species of beast and bird, of reptile and sea creature, can be tamed and has been tamed by the human species, but no one can tame the tongue—a restless evil, full of deadly poison."

Here, ironically, James listed the same categories of species that are listed in the book Genesis: beast and bird, reptile and sea creature. In Genesis, God gave humanity authority, and we were commanded to practice dominion over creatures. And for James, humans have successfully mastered this task. Yet, James exposed the fact that humans fail to practice control over their communications. What James wants us to realize is that it's sad that we can practice control over creatures, currency, careers, and compounds, but we lack control in our communication. Moreover, it becomes difficult to control our resources, responsibilities, and relationships if we lack control in our communication.

Cool Down

What topics of discussion always cause you to lose control in your communication? Why do you feel that you always respond in that way? This week, ask God for supernatural power and discipline to practice self-control in speech. Also, ask God to empower you with tools to help you maintain self-control.

Set 3: Untamed Tongues Contradict Christian Conduct

James concluded this pericope with a reality check. James offered in verses 9 and 10a, "With it we bless the Lord and Father, and with it we curse those who are made in the likeness of God. From the same mouth come blessing and cursing."

James's audience was a community of Messianic Jews who were indoctrinated with Jewish customs. It was custom for Jews to respond reverently with "blessed be He" whenever someone

mentioned or said the word *God*. This response became second nature. It was equivalent to some modern church colloquialisms that include "praise the Lord," "God is good . . . all the time—and all the time, God is good." These phrases are used commonly among many churchgoers.

Yet, through verses 9-10, James exposes the potential contradiction with the conduct of church-goers. James acknowledged that many church attendees specialize in blessing people and then cursing people with the same mouth and sometimes in the same breath. For James, this is a deplorable display of discipleship. For James, these actions contradict Christian conduct.

Discussion Question

How do you think nonbelievers view Christians when they witness them speaking positively and negatively on a consistent basis?

Notice James's words: with our mouths we bless the Lord and Father, and with it we curse those who are made in the likeness of God (see verse 9). Here, James reveals that the people toward whom we are malicious and the malevolent have been made in the likeness of God. The phrase "in the likeness" is the Greek word *Homoousios*, which means "of resemblance, similitude, or of similar substance." James confirms that we all have been made in the *Imago Dei*—the image of God. Thus, when we use our words to curse our brothers and sisters, we are cursing the very image of God and thus are cursing God. This is why Scripture reminds us, "Those who say, 'I love God,' and hate their brothers or sisters, are liars; for those who do not love a brother or sister whom they have seen, cannot love God whom they have not seen" (1 John 4:20).

Therefore, we must tame our tongues—we must practice control in communication; we must proclaim blessings with our words, because the way in which we treat people reveals the way in which we *love and honor God*.

 **Cool Down**

James reminded us that all people are made in the likeness of God. Now, what changes will you make to ensure that you are displaying your love for God by your treatment to God's people?

Final Stretch

1. How many times have you lost your witness due to a lack of self-control in speech?

_____

_____

_____

_____

2. How often do you view people as images of God when you are speaking to them?

_____

_____

_____

_____

3. In what ways could you adjust your speech to ensure that you are contributing positivity in all your conversations?

_____

_____

_____

_____

Session 11

People over Possessions

Lesson Focus Verses: *James 5:1-6*
Memory Verses: *Matthew 16:26; Mark 8:36; Luke 9:25*
Christian Virtue: *Prioritization*

Come now, you rich people, weep and wail for the miseries that are coming to you. Your riches have rotted, and your clothes are moth-eaten. Your gold and silver have rusted, and their rust will be evidence against you, and it will eat your flesh like fire. You have laid up treasure for the last days. Listen! The wages of the laborers who mowed your fields, which you kept back by fraud, cry out, and the cries of the harvesters have reached the ears of the Lord of hosts. You have lived on the earth in luxury and in pleasure; you have fattened your hearts in a day of slaughter. You have condemned and murdered the righteous one, who does not resist you. **(James 5:1-6)**

SESSION
11
Small-group Bible Study

Lesson Question

Why is it important for believers to value people more than possessions?

Lesson Objective

To understand that the believer's primary objective is to love God and love people. There are consequences to pay whenever people place the value of possessions above the lives of people.

 **Warm Up!**

Discussion Questions

- *What are your most prized possessions? What do you value the most?*
- *Have you ever been guilty of spending more time pursuing possessions than investing time into the people in your life?*

Word Study

Evidence *(martyrion)*: a witness or testimony; something evidential or testimonial.

Fraud *(apostereō)*: to rob or despoil; to make destitute; to deprive one thing or someone.

Miseries *(talaipōria)*: hardships, troubles, calamities, wretchedness.

Rotten *(sēpō)*: to make corrupt; to destroy.

 **Stretch It!**

As kingdom citizens, we all work to establish and advance the kingdom of God on Earth as it is in heaven. In order to achieve this goal, we must never place people over possessions.

It is true that God desires each disciple to be prosperous in his or her living, and the Word is clear on the promises of God, as discussed in the following verses:

- Malachi 3:10
- Psalm 37:25
- Philippians 4:19
- Deuteronomy 6:10-11; Joshua 24:13
- Proverbs 10:22

Discussion Questions

- *What happens when we become so consumed with acquiring assets that we forget or ignore the true purpose of discipleship?*
- *What is the purpose of discipleship?*

James writes to remind us that the sole purpose of discipleship is to fully love God and love people. The twelve tribes that James addressed were those who lived among societies that were heavily influenced by ultra-individualism, ultra-capitalism, and ultra-egocentricity. These factors promoted a culture that eagerly and unapologetically placed immense value on possessions—hence, diminishing the value of people.

Discussion Question
How has the present culture affected the way in which you value people and possessions?

James opened this passage by offering a warning to believers about the consequences of placing possessions as the chief priority in life.

James began his warning in verse 1: "Come now, you rich people, weep and wail for the miseries that are coming to you." This warning is addressed to *"rich people."* Now, James was not condemning the affluent solely on the basis of their abundant acquisitions. Conversely, James offers this warning to all people who have gained riches at the expense of others.

Yes, we have been given the promises of God—through the Word, which reminds us that *if we seek the kingdom of God and God's righteousness, then all things (which we desire, seek after, pursue, and work toward) will be added (given) to us* (see Matthew 6:33).

Discussion Question
Do we seek the kingdom and God's righteousness for "all the things that would be added," or do we seek the kingdom of God and God's righteousness simply because it is the kingdom?

James warns that those who place the value of possessions above people will experience miseries. The word *miseries* implies *hardships, troubles, calamities,* and *wretchedness.* Although this warning is a bit despairing for the "rich," it also reminds us about the grace of God. We are reminded that God always gives *a warning before destruction.* It is the job of the believer to heed the warning.

James continues by offering a detailed description of the miseries that will beset avaricious individuals. James warns about this in verses 2-3. Here, through James's warning, we all are given insight into the consequences of placing people over possessions.

The consequences of "the rich" include . . .

(1) _____

(2) _____

(3) _____

(4) _____

(5) _____

Through this warning, James echoed the sentiments of the Proverbs writer: *wealth is not profitable on a day of wrath, but righteousness rescues from death* (see Proverbs 11:4).

In the second phase of this warning, James explained the reasoning behind the promised punishment in verses 3-5. Here, James exposed the indictments against "the rich." These actions reveal the characteristics of those who place more value on possessions than people.

The consequences of "the rich" include . . .

(1) _____

(2) _____

(3) _____

By examining these mistakes, we are given some direction on how to value people over possessions.

(1) Make _____

(2) Make _____

(3) Make _____

Exercise It!

Set 1: Make Eternal Investments

James pens in verse 3b, "You have laid up treasure for the last days." Here, James revealed the nature of superficial individuals—people who only prioritize materialism.

Discussion Question

Why is it important to make meaningful investments into people's lives?

Remember the Hebrews writer's words that *every person has an appointed time to die* (see Hebrews 9:27). Indeed, we all will die. No one can escape the inevitability of death. You see, the superficial person spends his/her entire life seeking and sacrificing in order to obtain more temporal goods, not realizing that the most precious and prized assets on Earth are not store-bought items, but the individuals God places in our lives.

Discussion Questions

Could you imagine dying alone—without any family or friends by your side? How would that make you feel?

Remember Jesus' words: *no one knows the day or hour when He will return.* Beloved, remember: funeral hearses carry bodies but never carry U-Haul trucks filled with earthly goods. The lesson here is this: no one gets to take their earthly possessions with him or her when he or she dies. Believers must therefore commit themselves to making eternal investments on Earth. We achieve this goal by fully investing all our resources (time, talents, and treasures) into making extremely positive impacts on people's lives. Indeed, our earthly investments become eternal investments when we commit ourselves to valuing people above possessions.

 **Cool Down**

When you die, will people be able to honestly say, "He/she really positively impacted my life; I am grateful for what he/she invested in me"? This week, commit yourself to make several eternal investments into the lives of the people that God sends your way.

Set 2: Make Economic Decisions with Integrity

James summoned his audience with these words in verse 4: "Listen! The wages of the laborers who mowed your fields, which you kept back by fraud, cry out, and the cries of the harvesters have reached the ears of the Lord of hosts." In this text, the mentioned selfish individuals have spent their lives defrauding people.

The word *fraud* implies that this person robbed, despoiled, made destitute, and deprived someone. In our present context, these individuals would be akin to loan sharks, Ponzi Scheme representatives, and pyramid company agents.

God gives the world people and possessions. God expects us to love people and to use possessions to demonstrate that love. However, many people are guilty of loving possessions and using people to obtain those possessions.

Discussion Questions

Why should we refrain from taking advantage of people for personal gain? What are the dangers of living a life operating in this manner?

James warns that *the disenfranchised cry out and their cries have reached the ears of God* (see verse 4). This one verse reminds us all about the sovereignty and omniscience of God. We should practice integrity in all our economic decisions because God sees and knows all things. Jesus asks, "For what will it profit them if they gain the whole world but forfeit their life?" (Matthew 16:26a; see Mark 8:36 and Luke 9:25). Truly, we can spend our entire lives making poor temporary decisions that could have everlasting consequences. Therefore, we all should be careful to make sure that all our actions are pleasing in God's sight.

 **Cool Down**

Do you always practice integrity with your economic exploits? Have you ever been dishonest with the pursuit or the preservation of your finances? Have you ever mistreated someone or manipulated the system in order to gain more money or assets? If you are guilty of any of these, repent and ask God for grace and mercy for your mistakes. Second, ask God to transform your mind and to turn your heart to God's way. Lastly, ask God for favor and discipline as you commit yourself to righteous economic pursuits.

Set 3: Make Empathy a Matter of Importance

James concluded this portion of the pericope by exposing individuals who lack empathy. James argued, in verse 5, "You have lived on the earth in luxury and in pleasure; you have fattened your hearts in a day of slaughter." Here, James painted the picture of people who enjoy their riches, while enjoying the suffering of others.

Through this text, James exposed people who have allowed their fortunes to blind and numb them to the socio-economic disparities of the world. Here, we are reminded about the dire need for empathetic believers. Believers must work to erase famine, drought, disease, classism, racism, sexism, discrimination, oppression, bigotry, and hegemony. These issues play a significant role in the establishment and sustainability of the stronghold of poverty.

Discussion Question

Why is it important to respond to those in need?

Believers must practice having empathy for those in poverty because we all could be in that situation. Remember the words of Christ: "[God] makes his sun rise on the evil and on the good, and sends rain on the righteous and on the unrighteous" (Matthew 5:45). Indeed, everything we possess is by God's grace.

Reflect on Jesus' words in Matthew 25:45 and Paul's words in Acts 20:35.

 **Cool Down**

Have you allowed your success or the pursuit thereof to blind you and numb you from socio-economic ills? Each day this week, commit yourself to responding to at least one person who is in need. Ask God to lead you and equip you with the necessary resources so that you might make a huge impact on that person's life.

Final Stretch

1. How can you ensure that you consistently make eternal investments each day of your life?

_____

_____

_____

_____

2. What changes do you need to make in your life to ensure that all your economic pursuits are carried out with integrity?

_____

_____

_____

_____

3. What factors have you allowed to blind and numb you to all the socio-economic ills of the world? What changes can you make to ensure that you contribute to diminishing those factors?

_____

_____

_____

_____

SESSION 12

Be Patient!

Lesson Focus Verses: *James 5:7-12*
Memory Verse: *Romans 12:12*
Christian Virtue: *Patience*

Be patient, therefore, beloved, until the coming of the Lord. The farmer waits for the precious crop from the earth, being patient with it until it receives the early and the late rains. You also must be patient. Strengthen your hearts, for the coming of the Lord is near. Beloved, do not grumble against one another, so that you may not be judged. See, the Judge is standing at the doors! As an example of suffering and patience, beloved, take the prophets who spoke in the name of the Lord. Indeed we call blessed those who showed endurance. You have heard of the endurance of Job, and you have seen the purpose of the Lord, how the Lord is compassionate and merciful. Above all, my beloved, do not swear, either by heaven or by earth or by any other oath, but let your "Yes" be yes and your "No" be no, so that you may not fall under condemnation. **(James 5:7-12)**

Lesson Question

Why must believers practice patience?

Lesson Objective

To understand that patience is a chief characteristic of the fruit of the Spirit and that, moreover, when our patience is challenged, God uses these moments to establish and strengthen our faith in God and to develop Christian character.

 **Warm Up!**

Discussion Question

In what areas of your life are you the most impatient?

 **Stretch It!**

The main purpose of the book of James is to develop Christian virtue in the believers scattered across Asia Minor. One of the chief virtues of Christian discipleship is *patience*. Indeed, Christian disciples are called and expected to practice patience every day. Believers must practice patience, because patience is a characteristic of the fruit of the Spirit. Therefore, the presence of patience in one's life is one sign of the indwelling and the interworking of the Holy Spirit. Moreover, Scripture clearly states that love is patient. Thus, we display our love for people by practicing patience with them on a daily basis.

Word Study

Endurance *(hypomenō)*: take patiently; suffer; abide; tarry behind; to remain; not recede or flee; bear bravely and calmly.

Grumble *(stenazō)*: to sigh, groan, or murmur with grief or grudge.

Patience *(makrothymeō)*: bear long during offense and injurie; suffer long; long endurance during misfortunes and troubles; long spirit; to persevere.

Strengthen *(stērizō)*: establish; fix; steadfastly set; to make stable or place firmly.

James is relentless in developing the fruit of patience in these newly converted Messianic Christians. For James, patience is a necessity for every believer. James commands believers with these words in verse 7a: "Be patient, therefore, beloved, until the coming of the Lord." Here, *patience* indicates one who "bears and suffers long-term during offense and injuries." It also depicts "one who possesses long spirit and long endurance during misfortunes and troubles."

In short, patience implies _____ .

James used an illustration of a farmer to convey the importance of patience. James writes in verse 7b, "The farmer waits for the precious crop from the earth, being patient with it until it receives the early and the late rains."

We (believers) all are _____ .

This brilliant analogy connected the lives of believers to the lives of Palestinian farmers. Both communities depend on their work for sustenance and stability. The crops were the farmers' livelihood and the farmers' most valuable asset. The farmer would spend time and energy: sowing, plowing, watering, weeding, and chasing scavengers away from their yet-to-be-developed and harvested crops. Yet, even with all that work, the farmer still had to practice faith.

Similarly, since we are farmers, we *must practice faith as we toil the fields of life*. James informed us that farmers not only plant but also have to patiently wait for increase. With this illustration, James punctuates the fact that practicing faith requires an abundance of patience. Believers, therefore, must remain patient even while they are working and waiting to see increase in their lives.

Discussion Question
How do you handle moments when you are forced to wait?

Second, since we are farmers, we are reminded that our provisions and productivity come directly from our heavenly Father. James demonstrates our total dependency on God by analyzing the personal work of farmers. You see, some farmers possess advanced equipment and others own advanced technology that assist them in the agricultural work. However, all farmers need seed, soil, streams of rain, and sunshine in order for crops to grow. Farmers—no matter how skilled and equipped—depend on God for provisions and productivity. It is God who provides seed, soil, streams of rain, and sunshine for farmers. Paul reminds us that our faith rests not on human wisdom but on the power of God (see I Corinthians 2:5). Therefore, farmers—whether they recognize it or not, live by faith and are forced to practice patience during the wait. Indeed, trusting God's provisions in God's timing requires great patience. Likewise, we are dependent on God for provisions and productivity, and we must practice patience while we wait on God.

Discussion Questions

How frustrating is it to wait for God to make provisions in your life? How frustrated do you become when it feels like your life is unproductive?

James explained why believers must practice patience in the first section of this pericope. In the second section, James guides his audience on the proper way to practice patience.

Exercise It!

Set 1: We Must Strengthen Our Hearts

James commanded the believers with these words in verse 8b: "Strengthen your hearts." Here, the word *strengthen* means "to establish, to fix, to steadfastly set, or to make stable or place firmly." James commands believers to develop and maintain stability during moments when their patience is being challenged.

Notice, James's first focus is establishing stable hearts among believers. It is easy to lose physical, emotional, and spiritual stability when your faith is being challenged. This is why David encourages us to wait for the Lord; be strong and take heart and wait for the Lord (see Psalm 27:14). Believers must continue to establish, fix, steadfastly set, and stabilize the conditions of their hearts. This is extremely important, because our hearts serve as the hub for all our emotions, and our emotions control our actions. Moreover, it is easy for impatient people to make irrational decisions when they are suffering from spiritual and emotional instability.

_____ people usually make _____ decisions.

Discussion Questions

How important is it to maintain a strong heart during moments of impatience? How impactful is it to have someone to strengthen you during moments of difficulty?

James urges believers to maintain emotional stability while they are waiting on God, because our emotions—when fueled by impatience—will cause us to believe that God has not worked, is not working, or will not work on our behalf.

In order to deflate these deceptions, James encourages believers that the coming of the Lord is near (see verse 8). Here, James reminds his audience to be patient, because God never stops working on our behalf. Now, most theologians, when analyzing this word, conclude that James was speaking eschatologically (concerning the end times/the last of days) when he made this statement. This appears to be true. However, this statement also reminds the believer that God is working to ensure that His plans are manifested now and in the future to come. This reminder gives the believer hope that God is sovereign—God never forgets us—and it gives believers confidence that the one who began a good work in them will bring it to completion by the day of Jesus Christ (see Philippians 1:6).

 **Cool Down**

How have you allowed your impatience to cause you to make irrational decisions? Remember, it is important to remain stable during the moments when we have to wait on God. This week, ask God to strengthen your heart and ask God to empower you with unshakable confidence as you stand firmly on the promises of God.

Set 2: We Must Remain Positive

James continues with this command in verse 9a: "Beloved, do not grumble against one another." Here, James effectively captures and exposes a major hindrance to productivity and a chief toxin in every relationship. For James, *grumbling* stops the productivity in our lives, and *grumbling* poisons the relationships in our lives.

James admonishes the believers to eliminate *grumbling*, which means "to sigh, groan, or murmur with grief or grudge." The grumblers are the ones who allow their impatience to affect their attitudes and subsequent interactions with individuals.

Discussion Questions

Have you ever said something foul during a hostile or frustrating moment that you wish you could take back? How harmful were the effects of those words?

If we are honest, all of us have been guilty of allowing our impatience to cause us to grumble. Some of us grumble privately, and some of us grumble publicly; some of us grumble softly, and some of us grumble loudly; some of us grumble verbally, and some of us grumble electronically;

some of us grumble in person, and some of us grumble through social media. Still, all of us grumble, and grumbling is never productive.

Discussion Questions

Why shouldn't grumbling be allowed among believers? How dangerous are the effects of grumbling?

Scripture reminds us, "Whoever is patient has great understanding, but one who is quick-tempered displays folly" (Proverbs 14:29, NIV). Therefore, James explicitly orders his audience to rid themselves of all *grumbling*. James knew that grumbling and groaning very seldom assist or improve the quality of any situation—it only makes it worse. Indeed, most impatient criticisms are counterproductive, especially when everyone is under pressure. *Grumbling* only breeds havoc, rage, stagnation, regression, and ultimately, more impatience. Moreover, the time, breath, and energy that grumblers exert into negative groans could be applied to praying for the betterment of the situation.

Grumbling defects and destroys families, businesses, marriages, and ministries. This is why James instructed his audience to remove all aspects of *grumbling* within their community. You see, beloved, we must practice self-control and remain positive even during the challenging periods of our lives. It is impossible to develop the fruit of patience while *grumbling* along the way. We must learn how to use our moments of delay to cause us to grow closer to each other as we wait for God to manifest God's promises in our lives.

James cautioned *grumbling* believers with these words in verse 9: "Do not grumble against one another, so that you may not be judged. See, the Judge is standing at the doors!" Here, James reminded believers that *grumbling* not only damages our communities but also disturbs God—our Creator. With this explicit warning, we are reminded that God—the chief judge—observes all our actions. And if we grumble, we will have to give an account for all our actions and an account for the effects of those actions.

 Cool Down

How destructive have you been when you allowed your frustrations to cause you to grumble? Is there someone that you still owe an apology? This week, ask God to guide you as you seek to restore those fractured relationships. Also, ask God for the discipline to resist the urge to grumble in moments of delay and frustration moving forward.

Set 3: We Must Remember the Word of God

James concludes this section by offering support to believers who struggle with impatience. James proposes in verse 10, "As an example of suffering and patience, beloved, take the prophets who spoke in the name of the Lord." Here, James invites his audience to utilize the Word of God for reinforcement during the difficult days of deferment. You see, the Word of God is a *gift* that *guides* us through our faith journey. David echoed these sentiments with his declaration that the Word of God "is a lamp to my feet and light to my path" (Psalm 119:105).

Indeed, God's Word . . .

(1) _____.

(2) _____.

Discussion Question

How has the Word of God comforted you during your moments of impatience?

Through this invitation, James encourages believers to remember the Word of God. More importantly, James urged believers to recall the stories of the prophets who not only walked by faith but also had to practice patience through their faith journey. James wanted believers to know that the development of the virtue of patience is central to the Christian faith journey. Furthermore, James stressed that God would empower their community the same way that God empowered the prophets of Scripture. According to James, God's Word promises that when we practice patience and when we practice endurance, the Lord is compassionate and merciful.

 **Cool Down**

How deeply do you depend on the Word of God for direction in your life—particularly during moments of impatience? Do you seek the Word of God? Do you listen to and follow the Word of God? If you are experiencing impatience in an area of your life, ask God to strategically reveal a word in your life that will guide you and empower you.

Final Stretch

1. What areas of your life have left you with emotional instability? What changes do you need to make to regain stability in every area of your life?

_____

_____

_____

_____

2. What changes should you make to ensure that your words and actions are always positive during moments of frustration?

_____

_____

_____

_____

3. What steps are you taking to establish a more deeply biblically devoted life? Are there any distractions that you need to remove?

_____

_____

_____

_____

SESSION 13

Make Prayer
a Priority

Lesson Focus Verses: *James 5:13-20*
Memory Verse: *I Thessalonians 5:17*
Christian Virtue: *Prayer*

Are any among you suffering? They should pray. Are any
cheerful? They should sing songs of praise. Are any among
you sick? They should call for the elders of the church
and have them pray over them, anointing them with oil
in the name of the Lord. The prayer of faith will save the
sick, and the Lord will raise them up; and anyone who has
committed sins will be forgiven. Therefore confess your
sins to one another, and pray for one another, so that
you may be healed. The prayer of the righteous is powerful and effective. Elijah was a human being like us, and
he prayed fervently that it might not rain, and for three
years and six months it did not rain on the earth. Then
he prayed again, and the heaven gave rain and the earth
yielded its harvest. My brothers and sisters, if anyone
among you wanders from the truth and is brought back
by another, you should know that whoever brings back
a sinner from wandering will save the sinner's soul from
death and will cover a multitude of sins. **(James 5:13-20)**

Lesson Question

Why should disciples make prayer a priority?

Lesson Objective

To understand that when we properly prioritize prayer, our possibilities and promises are unlimited.

 **Warm Up!**

Discussion Questions

- *What are some very important aspects of relationships?*
- *How strong is your communication with God?*

 **Stretch It!**

God has given us a gift that unlocks His promises that are found in His Word. This is the gift of prayer. Unfortunately, although prayer is one of the most important tools for believers, it is often the most neglected tool in the believer's life.

Discussion Question

Why must believers value prayer?

Word Study

Effective *(energeō)*: to be operative, be at work, put forth power; to display one's activity; outward success.

Fervently *(proseuchē)*: prayer addressed to God; a place in the open air—outside the cities—outside the synagogue, where the Jews were not able to pray.

Righteous *(dikaios)*: just; right; observing divine laws; virtuous; keeping the commands of God; innocent, faultless, guiltless.

Believers must value and utilize the gift of prayer because Jesus established His earthly ministry upon the foundation of prayer. Prayer was the driving force of Jesus' life. In fact, the commencement of Jesus' earthly ministry (see Luke 4:1-13) and the conclusion of Jesus' earthly ministry (see Matthew 26:36-46) began with prayer. Moreover, prayer is one thing that Jesus extensively discussed with and explicitly taught His disciples (see Matthew 6:9-13). Jesus even plainly stated that some things only happen by prayer and fasting (see Matthew 17:21). Yes, all believers must follow the example of Christ: we all must value and fully devote ourselves to prayer.

We must also consider three things concerning prayer:

(1) Prayer is _____ . (John 15:7)

(2) Prayer _____ . (1 Thessalonians 5:17)

(3) Prayer _____ . (James 4:3)

James concluded this letter with a reminder to the believers about the importance of prayer.

Prayer must be a _____ in every believer's life.

Through this lesson, we will learn that we must make prayer a priority because . . .

(1) Prayer helps us _____ .

(2) Prayer helps us _____ .

(3) Prayer has _____ .

Exercise It!

Set 1: Prayer Helps Us Recognize People

James begins this discourse with a series of reflective rhetorical questions in verses 13 and 14: "Are any among you suffering? . . . Are any cheerful? . . . Are any among you sick?" Through these questions, James warns against the dangers of ignoring people. You see, prayer should not only *connect us with God* but also shape our *compassion for others*. Jesus desperately desired all His followers to practice showing compassion for the least, the lost, and the looked over. For James, prayer is one instrument that develops compassion among disciples.

The Zulu people of South Africa are the largest ethnic group in that country. The Zulu people have a remarkable salutation that they commonly use whenever they greet each other. Instead of uttering the most common "hello" of the Western culture, the Zulu people have popularized the greeting *"Sawubona,"* which simply means "I see you." This wonderful greeting reinforces the importance of community and communal awareness.

Similarly, believers are called to recognize people—to see and acknowledge others. Notice that each question James posed is prefaced with "are any among you . . .?" Indeed, prayer should cause us to examine our surroundings and identify the people that God has put into our lives. Through this text, we are reminded about three types of people that we must commit ourselves to recognizing.

Three types of people:

(1) _____

(2) _____

(3) _____

In the first place, James asked whether there was anyone among the people who was suffering. Now, James's categorization of "suffering" does not imply physical sickness; this suffering is associated with those who have been subjected to or those who are presently subject to unfair persecution.

In the second place, James asked whether there was anyone among them that was cheerful. Here, James identifies happy people. These are people who are of good spirits and cheer.

In the third place, James asked whether there was anyone among them that was sick. Here, the "sickness" implied includes *disease, feebleness,* and *impotence.* "Sickness" can also mean *weak in means or needy/poor.*

Discussion Question
Which category do you most associate with at this moment?

Please notice that James recognizes all these different people in the same breath. This is a reminder that it is very possible to have suffering, cheerful, and sick people all present within our communities and churches at the same. Therefore, James encourages believers to saturate themselves in prayer so that they may effectively recognize people and the predicaments that influence people.

 **Cool Down**

How well do you recognize the people in your life? How consistent are you in identifying people who are overtaken by a circumstance? This week, spend time in prayer and ask God to sharpen your awareness and sensitivity to the circumstances that beset the people around you.

Set 2: Prayer Helps Us Respond Properly to Predicaments

James urges believers to pray so that they may respond properly to the predicaments of the people.

James writes in verse 14, "Are any among you sick? They should call for the elders of the church and have them pray over them, anointing them with oil in the name of the Lord." Through this text, we are reminded that no one should be forced to endure problems alone. Conversely, God gives us community to help us navigate through our difficult times.

God will strategically send people our way who need our assistance during trying times. God has a track record of linking people together through difficult times; examples include these:

(1) _____

(2) _____

(3) _____

(4) _____

Discussion Questions

Has God ever sent someone to help you during a very difficult time in your life? How did that support help you persevere?

Indeed, God will deliberately assign people to us that we are called to aid in challenging times. Therefore, believers must remain prayerful so that they may be equipped to assist those in need.

James offers a simplistic and practical solution. James writes in verse 14, "Are any among you sick? They should call for the elders of the church and have them pray over them, anointing them with oil in the name of the Lord."

The believers' proper response to predicaments:

(1) Believers must _____

(2 Believers must _____

James reminded his audience about two simple yet powerful ministries in which everyone must engage:

(1) The ministry of _____

(2) The ministry of _____

In our text, James instructed the sick to call for the elders of the church. It is important for us to make time to be present with people during difficult days and times.

One of the best demonstrations of the ministry of presence is captured in Job 2:11-13. Truly, sometimes people just want to know that you care enough to be with them through life's agony.

Discussion Statement/Question
Recall a time when someone's presence meant the world to you. How important is it to have someone present with you during tormenting and isolated moments?

Remember, James already informed us that *faith without works is dead.* Our faith is activated through our actions toward one another. We do not have to function as 'messiahs'; we already have one and his name is Jesus. We are only expected to practice compassion.

 **Cool Down**

When is the last time you immediately stopped everything and went to be present with some-one after hearing about his/her poor predicament? Are there people in your life who would be empowered by your presence? This week, ask God for the compassion to be present with peo-ple in need. Also, ask God to help you restructure your schedule so that you can become more consistent with this task.

Discussion Question

So, what happens when believers make prayer a priority?

Set 3: Prayer Has Results for Those Who Practice It

James concludes this portion of Scripture by reminding his audience about the results of prayer. James contended that "the prayer of the righteous is powerful and effective" (James 5:16b).

Here, the word *effective* means "to be operative, to be at work, to put forth power, to display one's activity, which produces outward success." James is clear that God responds to the prayers of the righteous.

In fact, James cemented his claim concerning the effectiveness of righteous prayers in verses 15-18.

For James, when the righteous pray, . . .

(1) _____

(2) _____

(3) _____

Indeed, all believers should pray for those in need with full assurance that God hears and will respond to them.

 **Cool Down**

In your estimation, how powerful and effective are your prayers? Have you ever witnessed the miraculous works of prayer? Is your faint prayer life indicative of your lack of faith? This week, commit yourself to reigniting your passion in prayer and your faith in the results of prayer.

Final Stretch

1. How can you become more sensitive to the circumstances of the people in your life?

_____

_____

_____

_____

2. What small changes could you make to ensure that you have more time to be present with people in need?

_____

_____

_____

_____

3. What is holding you back from fully trusting God to respond to your prayers?

_____

_____

_____

_____

LEADER'S GUIDE INSTRUCTIONS: For each session, refer to the student components for insight into the text. Any new information or teacher instructions will appear in this section.

Session 1 • Small-group Bible Study • Leader's Guide

I Have Joy

Lesson Focus Verses: *James 1:2-4*
Memory Verse: *Nehemiah 8:10*
Christian Virtue: *Joy*

Warm Up!

During discussion related to the "Warm Up!" section, display different pictures of smiling faces. Consider using emojis. Also, find a song that emphasizes happiness and play a few seconds of that song.

Ask: What makes you happy?

Identify: Most people find happiness through… *resources* (what we have), *relationships* (who we have), and *responsibilities* (what we do).

Explain: Seeking happiness through resources, relationships, and responsibilities is not always fulfilling. In fact, sometimes, the acquisition of these things only frustrates us more.

Ask: In which category do you usually seek happiness, and why?

Discuss: Feelings of happiness are temporary, while the experience of joy is permanent. Moreover, feelings of happiness are situational; however, the experience of joy is relational. You see, the attainment of joy is contingent upon one's relationship with Jesus. We never remain the same after we experience the joy of the Lord.

Connect: The problems and pressures of life are inevitable—we will all experience them. However, God's joy empowers us to persevere past the persecutions of life.

Stretch It!

Fill-in-the-Blank Answers: We not only need the right <u>actions</u>; we also need the right <u>attitudes</u>. Our attitudes affect our … <u>actions</u> and <u>attributes</u>.

Explain: You see, God <u>allows us to be tested</u>, and the Enemy <u>seeks to tempt us</u>.

Exercise It!

Discuss: In the first movement, James identified the problem that might prevent our joy.

Set 1: Do Not Let Problems Stop You
After reading James 1:2, please notice James's words: WHEN you face trials of any kind.

Discuss: Only believers can find strength and stability on difficult and devastating days. The Holy Spirit equips believers with unspeakable joy—a joy that empowers believers to overcome every opposition.

Cool Down

Discuss: The second thing we must realize is that God produces perseverance through our problems.

Set 2: Let God Produce Perseverance
Explain: Indeed, "Our persecution is <u>temporary</u>, but our joy is <u>permanent</u>."

At the end of Set 2, discuss this: "The last thing we must realize is that promotion always follows production."

Set 3: God Prospers after God Produces
Discuss: According to James, God prospers believers by making them <u>perfect</u>, <u>complete</u>, and <u>sufficient</u>.

Final Stretch

Encourage the students to respond to the questions/statements posed in this section. Lead a discussion.

Session 2 • Small-group Bible Study • Leader's Guide

Wisdom: The Missing Ingredient

Lesson Focus Verses: *James 1:5-8*
Memory Verse: *Psalm 11:10*
Christian Virtue: *Wisdom*

Warm Up!

During discussion related to the "Warm Up!" section, display a bowl with ingredients used to make a cake.

Ask: What ingredients does it take to make a great cake?

Identify: We all have different ingredients that we believe are essential for baking the best cake. However, sometimes, we can miss something during the process.

Ask: Have you ever baked/cooked something and after tasting the finished product, you discovered that something was missing?

Explain: We all have been in a place where we felt like we were missing something.

Discuss: Most people spend their entire lives seeking pleasures, wealth, and prestige, only to discover that their lives are missing something. Many people fail to seek the missing ingredient—wisdom—as they concern themselves with the acquisition and maintenance of superficial things. Unfortunately, without wisdom, it becomes very difficult to garner the discipline needed in order to manage all that we obtain.

Connect: God eagerly waits to give us wisdom to help us as we navigate through life. However, we must be willing to seek after wisdom, and we must be willing to ask God for wisdom by faith. We will prosper beyond measure when we embrace the wisdom of God.

Stretch It!

Discuss: Here, James indicates that "the missing ingredient is <u>wisdom</u>."

Completed Statement: The ingredient that every believer must possess is <u>wisdom</u>!

Exercise It!

Say: First, James charges us to seek wisdom.

Set 1: Seek Wisdom
Completed Statement: Wisdom is <u>the capacity to see things from God's perspective and the ability to maturely respond according to scriptural principles</u>.

Discuss: Seeds of wisdom always leave long-lasting impacts on our lives. The gift of wisdom gives direction that helps people traverse through life.

Fill-in-the-Blank Answers: The benefits of wisdom include <u>Discernment</u>, <u>Direction</u>, <u>Discipline</u>.

Discuss: Second, James reminds us that God gives wisdom.

Set 2: Ask for Wisdom
Fill-in-the-Blank Answers: James is clear that God gives <u>generously</u>, <u>ungrudgingly</u>.

Discuss: In the third place, James charges us to ask for wisdom.

Set 4: Apply Wisdom
The four essentials:

(1) <u>Meditate on God's Word</u> (Psalm 1:1-3)

(2) <u>Observe God's works in the world</u> (Proverbs 6:6)

(3) <u>Associate with wise people</u> (Proverbs 13:20)

(4) <u>Heed to godly counsel</u> (Proverbs 12:15)

Final Stretch

Encourage the students to respond to the questions/statements posed in this section. Lead a discussion.

Session 3 • Small-group Bible Study • Leader's Guide

Overcoming Shallowness

Lesson Focus Verses: *James 1:9-11*
Memory Verse: *Proverbs 11:4*
Christian Virtue: *Maturity*

Warm Up!

During discussion related to the "Warm Up!" section, display a local lottery logo or images of a popular game show where contestants win massive amounts of money.

Ask: What would you buy if you won the lottery, the jackpot, or a game-show prize?

Identify: We typically desire and seek after things such as cars, cash, clothes, homes, electronics, jewelry, etc.

Explain: Although these things are desired and heavily pursued, they don't last long.

Ask: Have you ever spent a lot of money on something that didn't last very long?

Discuss: Most people spend their entire lives seeking shallow, superficial possessions that will eventually depreciate and deteriorate over time. Instead, we should have a desire to pursue more than that.

Connect: We may never hit the lotto, win a jackpot, or win a prize on a television game; however, God has promised to shower us with His riches in glory if we are willing to overcome the shallowness in the pursuit of superficialities.

Stretch It!

Discuss: Unfortunately, since people find value and self-worth in assets, many people seek <u>the hand</u> of God instead of <u>the heart</u> of God.

Exercise It!

Explain: In the first place, James encouraged us to boast about godly riches.

Set 1: Boast about Godly Riches
Discuss: You see, we should never boast about <u>our goods</u>; we should only boast about <u>God's goodness</u>.

Explain: Believers do not boast about <u>earthly</u> riches; believers boast about <u>godly</u> riches.

Discuss: James warns us to never trust the temporal.

Set 2: Never Trust the Temporal
After discussing the text in Set 2, say, "In the last place, James encourages us to invest in eternity."

Set 3: Invest in Eternity
Explain: In these two verses, James makes two things very clear:
(1) <u>Death is inevitable</u>.
(2) <u>Dividends are not eternal</u>.

Explain: Our only true <u>security</u> is found in our <u>salvation</u>.

Say: We are given an eternal investment plan for believers in I Timothy 6:17-18 (NIV): "Command those who are rich in this present world not to be arrogant nor to put their hope in wealth, which is so uncertain, but to put their hope in God, who richly provides us with everything for our enjoyment. Command them to do good, to be rich in good deeds, and to be generous and willing to share."

Discuss: According to I Timothy 6:17-18, we invest in eternity when we . . .
(1) <u>hope in God</u>;
(2) <u>do good</u>;
(3) <u>are rich in good deeds</u>;
(4) <u>are generous</u>;
(5) <u>are willing to share</u>.

Explain: The writer concludes with these words in I Timothy 6:19 (NIV): "In this way they will lay up treasure for themselves as a firm foundation for the coming age, so that they may take hold of the life that is truly life."

Final Stretch
Encourage the students to respond to the questions/statements posed in this section. Lead a discussion.

Session 4 • Small-group Bible Study • Leader's Guide

Fighting Temptations

Lesson Focus Verse: *James 1:13-15*
Memory Verse: *1 Corinthians 10:13*
Christian Virtue: *Discipline*

Warm Up!

During discussion related to the "Warm Up!" section, display the phrase "Guilty Pleasures" on a board or screen, or via handouts.

Ask: What are your guilty pleasures?

Identify: Most people are tempted in the areas of food, sex, and drugs (legal and illegal).

Explain: Many people become weak and fall victim to these temptations because they all offer physical satisfaction. Indeed, we are lured in by desires of satisfaction.

Show students a fishing lure, then ask, "What's the purpose of this lure?"

Discuss: Lures are designed to help people catch fish. If a fisher has the right bait, lures can attract fish and even force them out of hiding places. Fish can become so attracted to bait and lures that they fail to realize they are hanging by hooks until it is too late to shake free.

Connect: We all are lured, attracted, and baited by our weaknesses in life. James used the fishing-lure imagery to convey how our desires and our temptations lure us into sin. Just like with fish, sin sometimes seems attractive until we are left with the pain of hooks.

Stretch It!

Discuss: Our two greatest threats: <u>self</u> and <u>Satan</u>.

Explain: Sin literally means "<u>to miss the mark</u>." Moreover, sin is the willful, voluntary, and intentional disregard and disobedience to the Word of God in both word and deed. Let's be honest and address the seemingly often-ignored elephant in the room—sin is real, and everyone struggles with sin! Indeed, we all struggle with sin, whether we acknowledge it or not.

Discuss: There are two major manifestations of sin that we encounter each day: sins of <u>commission</u> and sins of <u>omission</u>.

Exercise It!

Explain: The first thing we must realize is that we make excuses.

Set 1: Do Not Make Excuses
Explain: It is true that God <u>tests</u> and Satan <u>tempts</u>.

After reading the text in Set 1, say, "The second thing we must realize is that we are moved by what excites us."

Set 2: Do Not Be Moved by What Excites You
Deception
Prior to reading the "deception" text in Set 2, display the fishing hook and bait.

Explain: The last thing we must realize is that we miss the exit.

Set 3: Do Not Miss the Exit
Explain: First Corinthians 10:13 states, "No testing has overtaken you that is not common to everyone. God is faithful, and he will not let you be tested beyond your strength, but with the testing he will also provide the way out so that you may be able to endure it."

*Display a picture of an exit ramp, then say, "Remember: The exit of deliverance always comes through the Word of God."

Explain: We must . . .

(1) <u>receive</u> the Word.

(2) <u>respond</u> to the Word.

(3) <u>reproduce</u> the Word.

Final Stretch

Encourage the students to respond to the questions/statements posed in this section. Lead a discussion.

Session 5 • Small-group Bible Study • Leader's Guide

Be Grateful

Lesson Focus Verses: *James 1:16-18*
Memory Verse: *James 1:17*
Christian Virtue: *Gratefulness*

Warm Up!

Before discussion related to the "Warm Up!" section, play a song about gratefulness. Consider "Be Grateful" by Walter Hawkins or "Grateful" by Hezekiah Walker.

Ask: For what are you most grateful?

Explain: We have a tendency to allow our day-to-day activities to distract us from so many of the blessings that we enjoy each day.

Discuss: We must never forget that God is the source of all our blessings, and we must never forget to express our gratitude for all that God does in our lives.

Connect: God desires for all of us to walk gratefully with the confidence that we serve a sovereign God who supplies all our needs every single day.

Exercise It!

Explain: In the first place, James reminds us that God is our source.

Set 1: Be Grateful that God Is Your Source
Explain: Consequently, we typically credit our success to . .
(1) <u>Experience/Expertise</u>.
(2) <u>Education</u>.
(3) <u>Associations/Affiliations</u>.

Explain: Indeed, God is both <u>the gift</u> and <u>the giver</u>.

Explain: Here, James informed his audience that God gives <u>generously</u> and <u>perfectly</u>.

After reading the text in Set 1, say, "In the second place, James reminds us that God is sovereign."

Set 2: Be Grateful that God Is Sovereign

Explain: James rallies all of us to express our gratitude for a God who is and will always be the sovereign one who supplies all our <u>needs according to God's riches in glory</u> (see Philippians 4:19).

Explain: God always keeps His promises. Therefore, we are to be grateful that God not only showers us continuously and repeatedly, but also that God never changes.

After reading the text in Set 2, say, "In the last place, James reminds us that God sent the Son."

Set 3: Be Grateful that God Sent the Son

Discuss: We are grateful that

(1) God is the <u>greatest giver</u>.

(2) God gives <u>the greatest gifts</u>.

(3) God gave us the <u>greatest gift: Jesus</u>.

Final Stretch

Encourage the students to respond to the questions/statements posed in this section. Lead a discussion.

Session 6 • Small-group Bible Study • Leader's Guide

Pressure Points

Lesson Focus Verse: *James 1:19-21*
Memory Verse: *James 1:19*
Christian Virtue: *Self-control*

Warm Up!

During discussion related to the "Warm Up!" section, display different hurtful phrases on a board.

Ask: How do these phrases make you feel? How have you reacted when people have said these things to you?

Identify: Our discomfort and disdain toward these phrases are triggers known as pressure points.

Explain: When we do not practice self-control, we are subject to fall victim to the reactions from our pressure points' being pushed.

Ask: Have you ever spoken too soon? Have you ever said something in the moment that you really did not mean? Have you ever said something you wish you could take back?

Discuss: God never wants us to be controlled by our pressure points.

Connect: We can gain control over our pressure points because we have parted ways with our past, and we now walk in the newness of Christ. God empowers us with His implanted Word so that we may continue to produce God's righteousness.

Stretch It!

Related to the "Stretch It!" Section, explain that there is a strong correlation between <u>salvation</u>, <u>servitude</u>, and <u>self-control</u>.

Explain: Our words can either <u>build</u> or <u>break</u>.

Exercise It!

Explain: In the first movement, James commands us to practice self-control.

Set 1: Practice Self-control

Explain: Here, James introduced a three-step self-control formula:

(1) <u>Listen</u>

(2) <u>Learn</u>

(3) <u>Love</u>

After reading the text in Set 1, say, "In the second place, James directs us to produce God's righteousness."

Set 2: Produce God's Righteousness

Explain: Our <u>actions of anger</u> are never <u>productive actions</u>.

After reading the text in Set 2, say, "In the last place, James reminds us to part ways with our past."

Set 3: Part Ways with Your Past

Explain: Here, James is clear: If we want to practice self-control, and if we want to produce God's righteousness, then we must <u>part</u> ways with our <u>past</u> ways.

Final Stretch

Encourage the students to respond to the questions/statements posed in this section. Lead a discussion.

Session 7 • Small-group Bible Study • Leader's Guide

Practice What You Preach

Lesson Focus Verses: *James 1:22-25*
Memory Verse: *John 15:7*
Christian Virtue: *Obedience*

Warm Up!

During discussion related to the "Warm Up!" section, display a large mirror.

Ask: What physical qualities do you most like about yourself?

Identify: Mirrors not only reveal the qualities that we like, but they also expose the areas in which we wish we could improve.

Ask: What physical qualities do you wish you could alter about yourself?

Explain: God's Word is a gift to the world. The Word of God is the mirror into our lives. The Word of God exposes our flaws, and it also empowers us to make the necessary changes for spiritual development and prosperity.

Discuss: Unfortunately, many people either ignore or reject the revelations from the mirror of God's Word.

Connect: God equipped us with the Word of God so that we might receive the Word, reflect on the Word, and replicate the Word. God promises to bless not only all who hear the Word but also all who practice the Word.

Stretch It!

Explain: In our text today, James offered three mandates for believers:

(1) We must <u>receive</u> the Word of God.

(2) We must <u>reflect</u> on the Word of God.

(3) We must <u>replicate</u> the Word of God.

Exercise It!

Explain: First, we must receive the Word of God.

Set 1: Receive the Word

Explain: We receive the Word through:

(1) <u>public designated times of worship</u>.

(2) <u>personal devotion</u>.

After reading the text in Set 1, say, "Second, we must reflect on the Word."

Set 2: Reflect on the Word

Explain: First, through this metaphor, we are reminded that the Word of God is the <u>mirror</u> into our lives.

Explain: Forgetfulness is not <u>ignorance</u>; it is blatant <u>insubordination</u>.

Explain: The Word does not <u>simply inform</u>; the Word is designed to <u>transform</u>. Indeed, God desires to transform our lives through the Word of God.

After reading the text in Set 2, say, "Lastly, we must replicate the Word."

Set 3: Replicate the Word

Explain: We must

(1) <u>acknowledge</u> God's Word.

(2) <u>accept</u> God's Word.

(3) <u>apply</u> God's Word.

Final Stretch

Encourage the students to respond to the questions/statements posed in this section. Lead a discussion.

Session 8 • Small-group Bible Study • Leader's Guide

Be Fair

Lesson Focus Verses: *James 2:1-13*
Memory Verse: *James 2:13*
Christian Virtue: *Equality*

Warm Up!

During discussion related to the "Warm Up!" section, display a list of popular movies, music genres/artists, sport teams, holidays, or seasons.

Ask: What's your favorite, and why?

Identify: We all have our various reasons for loving our favorites. We can agree that we all treat our favorites differently than all others.

Explain: Sometimes, practicing favoritism can be problematic. We cause problems when we show favoritism among people.

Ask: Have you ever been treated unfairly because you weren't someone's favorite?

Discuss: Showing favoritism among people is unfair, and it always leaves someone hurt.

Connect: Believers should always treat everyone equally. Those who love God should never alienate anyone. In fact, to show favoritism among people is a direct contradiction to the law of God given to us through Jesus, which is to love your neighbor as yourself.

Exercise It!

Explain: In the first movement, James reminds believers that discrimination denies godly living.

Set 1: Discrimination Denies Godly Living
Explain: Before we continue, we must recognize that we are the church. We are the ecclesia/ekklesia—the "called-out ones."

Say: Tell yourself: I am <u>the church</u>.

After reading the text in Set 1, say, "The second thing we must realize is that discrimination dishonors God's people."

Set 2: Discrimination Dishonors God's People

Explain: The two types of people described represent <u>the privileged</u> and <u>the poor</u>.

Explain: Discrimination begins with <u>evil thoughts</u>.

Explain: To <u>dishonor God's people</u> is to <u>dishonor God</u>.

Explain: We must remember that what we do toward <u>people</u> is what we do toward <u>God</u>.

After reading the text in Set 2, say, "The last thing we must realize is that discrimination defies God's Word."

Final Stretch

Encourage the students to respond to the questions/statements posed in this section. Lead a discussion.

Session 9 • Small-group Bible Study • Leader's Guide

Faith in Action: Show It!

Lesson Focus Verses: *James 2:14-20, 26*
Memory Verse: *James 2:26*
Christian Virtue: *Compassion*

Warm Up!

During discussion related to the "Warm Up!" section, display the words *poverty, famine, drought, homelessness,* and *sickness.*

Ask: How do you feel about these words?

Identify: Most people are sensitive and feel terrible about these issues.

Ask: What would you do/what are you doing to help impact and eliminate these issues?

Explain: Many believers pray and believe for the removal of these unfortunate circumstances. However, very few act to ensure that this becomes a reality.

Discuss: Believers are called to respond to the ills and issues of the world with our works. If we fail to act, then our faith stands inactive.

Connect: Our faith requires action—an action to protect those who are hurt, harmed, and in poor health. Our faith-activated actions have longer-lasting impacts on people than mere proclamations. We must put our faith in action—we must show it!

Stretch It!

Explain: James seeks to contrast two types of faith: (1) <u>living</u> faith; (2) <u>dead</u> faith.

Explain: In our text today, James offers three reasons for why we must put our faith in action:
(1) Faith without action does not <u>protect</u>.
(2) Faith without action does not <u>provide</u>.
(3) Faith without action does not <u>produce</u>.

Exercise It!

Explain: In the first place, James argues that faith without action does not protect.

Set 1: Faith without Action Does Not Protect
After reading the text in Set 1, say, "Second, James reminds us that faith without action does not provide."

Set 2: Faith without Action Does Not Provide
Explain: We must not only <u>proclaim blessings</u>; we must <u>also practice benevolence</u>.

After reading the text in Set 2, say, "Lastly, James maintains that faith without action does not produce."

Set 3: Faith without Action Does Not Produce
Explain: In a real sense, we have to <u>produce</u> what we <u>proclaim</u>.

Explain: Jesus reminded us that <u>our fruit</u> validates <u>our faith</u>.

Final Stretch

Encourage the students to respond to the questions/statements posed in this section. Lead a discussion.

Session 10 • Small-group Bible Study • Leader's Guide

Tame the Tongue

Lesson Focus Verses: *James 3:1-12*
Memory Verse: *Proverbs 18:21*
Christian Virtue: *Gentleness*

Warm Up!
During discussion related to the "Warm Up!" section, display sticks and stones.

Ask: Who remembers the saying, "sticks and stones may break my bones…"? (*Let the class finish the statement.*)

Identify: This old adage has been used for years to teach children about the importance of overcoming verbal abuse. Indeed, those who overcome verbal abuse are unstoppable.

Explain: It is true that it is possible to overcome verbal abuse. However, sometimes, malicious words can have everlasting negative impacts on the people that fall victim to the venomous sprays.

Ask: How have evil words negatively impacted your life?

Discuss: Many people fail to practice self-control in speech and are guilty of spewing vile words that, unfortunately, have long-lasting, destructive impacts on people's lives.

Connect: God expects believers to practice self-control in speech. Believers must learn how to tame their tongues if they wish to effectively represent and advance the kingdom of God.

Stretch It!
Explain:
(1) Words are <u>weapons</u>.
(2) Words cannot be <u>wiped away</u>.
(3) Words are <u>our witness</u>.

Explain: Through this, we learn that mature people are those who have <u>mastered controlling their mouths.</u>

Exercise It!

Explain: In the first movement, James warns that untamed tongues contaminate us.

Set 1: Untamed Tongues Contaminate
Explain: Here, James warns that even though the tongue is <u>small</u>, the tongue is <u>powerful</u>.

Explain: According to James, the untamed tongue contaminates us because . . .

(1) The untamed tongue <u>is situated in our place</u>.

(2) The untamed tongue <u>stains our people</u>.

(3) The untamed tongue <u>scourges our productivity</u>.

Explain: The second thing we must realize is that untamed tongues control us.

Set 2: Untamed Tongues Control
Explain: Our words can either direct us toward our <u>destiny</u> or our <u>demise</u>.

Explain: The last thing we must realize is that untamed tongues contradict Christian conduct.

Final Stretch

Encourage the students to respond to the questions/statements posed in this section. Lead a discussion.

Session 11 • Small-group Bible Study • Leader's Guide

People over Possessions

Lesson Focus Verses: *James 5:1-6*
Memory Verses: *Matthew 16:26; Mark 8:36; Luke 9:25*
Christian Virtue: *Prioritization*

Warm Up!

During discussion related to the "Warm Up!" section, display several pictures of expensive cars, clothes, homes, jewelry, and electronics.

Ask: What are your most prized possessions? What do you value the most?

Identify: Typically, most people find the greatest value in their material possessions.

Explain: Many people spend their entire lives pursuing materialistic possessions—sometimes at the expense of people—only to discover that those possessions are temporal.

Ask: Have you ever been guilty of spending more time pursuing possessions than investing time into the people in your life?

Discuss: Every believer must realize that God will bless us; however, discipleship and kingdom advancement are not found in what we can acquire and obtain; they are measured in how intentional we are about valuing and loving people.

Connect: God's Word warns us that materialistic possessions are temporal. Second, God's Word informs us that there are major consequences associated with those who decide to put more value on possessions than on the value of people.

Stretch It!

Explain: The consequences of being one of "the rich" include . . .

(1) Your riches will rot.

(2) Your resources will be removed.

(3) Your gold and silver will rust.

(4) You wrongs will be revealed.

(5) Your guilt will rip you apart.

Explain: The charges of "the rich" include . . .

(1) <u>They build a foundation on stuff</u>.

(2) <u>They practice fraudulent activity</u>.

(3) <u>They are satisfied with fortunes while others suffer</u>.

Explain: By examining these mistakes, we are given some direction on how to value people over possessions.

(1) Make <u>eternal investments</u>.

(2) Make <u>economic decisions with integrity</u>.

(3) Make <u>empathy a matter of importance</u>.

Exercise It!

Explain: In the first movement, James instructs us to make eternal investments.

Set 1: Make Eternal Investments

Explain: Second, James directs us to make economic decisions with integrity.

Set 2: Make Economic Decisions with Integrity

Explain: Lastly, James commands us to make empathy a matter of importance.

Final Stretch

Encourage the students to respond to the questions/statements posed in this section. Lead a discussion.

Session 12 • Small-group Bible Study • Leader's Guide

Be Patient!

Lesson Focus Verses: *James 5:7-12*
Memory Verse: *Romans 12:12*
Christian Virtue: *Patience*

Warm Up!

During discussion related to the "Warm Up!" section, display a pot full of water.

Ask: Have you ever heard the saying "a watched pot never boils"?

Identify: Most people struggle with impatience. We all hate waiting: in traffic, in restaurants, in stores, in parking lots, in relationships, in business, and in life overall. We want everything right now.

Ask: In what areas of your life are you the most impatient?

Discuss: We are heavily influenced by the fast-paced society that usually delivers everything we want in a matter of seconds/minutes. Convenience is everything. There are multiple businesses, websites, social-media outlets, and phone applications that specialize in connecting us with as little wait time as possible.

Connect: Unfortunately, the faith journey is not always fast-paced. God has a track record of making believers wait on God's timing. Patience is a chief characteristic of the fruit of the Spirit. Therefore, God requires for all believers to possess and practice the fruit of patience. Moreover, when our patience is challenged, God uses these moments to establish and strengthen our faith in God and to develop Christian character.

Stretch It!

Explain: In short, patience implies <u>perseverance. This is the mandate for every believer.</u>

Explain: Here, through this agrarian illustration, James exposed a reality for all believers: we all are <u>farmers.</u>

Exercise It!

Explain: First, while we wait, we must strengthen our hearts.

Set 1: We Must Strengthen Our Hearts
Explain: <u>Impatient</u> people usually make <u>irrational</u> decisions.

Explain: Second, while we wait, we must remain positive.

Set 2: We Must Remain Positive
Explain: Lastly, while we wait, we must remember the Word of God.

Set 3: We Must Remember the Word of God
Explain: God's Word . . .
(1) <u>directs us during the wait</u>.
(2) <u>teaches us discipline during the wait</u>.

Final Stretch

Encourage the students to respond to the questions/statements posed in this section. Lead a discussion.

Session 13 • Small-group Bible Study • Leader's Guide

Make Prayer a Priority

Lesson Focus Verses: *James 5:13-20*
Memory Verse: *1 Thessalonians 5:17*
Christian Virtue: *Prayer*

Warm Up!

Ask: What are some very important aspects of relationships?

Identify: Most relationship experts agree that communication is the most important aspect of any relationship.

Discuss: Prayer is communication and communion with God. Although prayer is one of the most important tools for believers, it is often the most neglected tool in the believer's life.

Ask: How strong is your communication with God?

Connect: God desires for all people to pray—to communicate with God. Prayer strengthens our relationship with God and fortifies our faith in Him. Furthermore, prayer reinforces the disciplines of our Christian faith. Prayer helps us recognize people and to respond properly to predicaments. Lastly, God promises to reward those who practice the discipline of prayer.

Stretch It!

Explain: Prayer must be a priority in every believer's life.

Explain: Through this lesson, we will learn that we must make prayer a priority because
(1) Prayer helps us <u>recognize people</u>.
(2) Prayer helps us <u>respond properly to predicaments</u>.
(3) Prayer has <u>rewards for those who practice it</u>.

Exercise It!

Explain: First, we learn that prayer helps us recognize people.

Set 1: Prayer Helps Us Recognize People
Explain: Through this text, we are reminded about three types of people that we must commit ourselves to recognizing:

(1) Hurt people
(2) Happy people
(3) People who need healing

Explain: Second, we learn that prayer helps us respond properly to predicaments.

Set 2: Prayer Helps Us Respond Properly to Predicaments
Explain: God has a track record of linking people together through difficult times:
(1) Naomi had Ruth.
(2) David had Jonathan.
(3) Paul had Silas.
(4) Daniel had Shadrach, Meshach, and Abednego.

Explain: These are the believers' proper responses to predicaments:
(1) Believers must be present.
(2) Believers must pray.

Explain: James reminded his audience about two simple yet powerful ministries in which everyone must engage:
(1) The ministry of presence
(2) The ministry of prayer

Ask: So, what happens when believers make prayer a priority?

Explain: Lastly, we learn that prayer has results for those who practice it.

Set 3: Prayer Has Results for Those Who Practice It
Explain: For James, when the righteous pray . . .
(1) The sick are saved and raised up.
(2) The sinful are forgiven and healed.
(3) The miraculous is performed to validate our faith.

Final Stretch
Encourage the students to respond to the questions/statements posed in this section. Lead a discussion.

Notes

Notes

Notes

Notes

CPSIA information can be obtained
at www.ICGtesting.com
Printed in the USA
LVHW100522040820
662292LV00005B/107

9 781949 052077